"One Grand Pursuit":

A Brief History Of The American Philosophical Society's First 250 Years, 1743-1993

Frontispiece. Benjamin Franklin. Oil portrait on canvas by Charles Willson Peale, copy after David Martin's 1767 portrait, 1772 (American Philosophical Society). Photography by Frank Margeson.

"One Grand Pursuit":

A Brief History Of The American Philosophical Society's First 250 Years, 1743-1993

By
EDWARD C. CARTER II

The experience of ages shows that improvements of a public nature are best carried on by societies of liberal and ingenious men uniting their labours, without regard to nation, sect or party, in one grand pursuit.

From the Society's Charter of March 15, 1780

American Philosophical Society • Philadelphia • 1993

Contents

List of Illustrations vii

Preface ix

Some General Observations 1

Creating the Society, 1743-1790 11

The New Nation's Scientific
    Society, 1790-1848 19

The Quiet Years, 1848-1900 33

Renewal and Redefinition, 1900-1942 51

The Modern Society, 1942-1993 83

Things to Come 109

Hail But Not Farewell 113

Sources Cited 115

Selected Bibliography 117

List of Illustrations

Cover. Thomas Jefferson. Plaster bust from the original by Jean Antoine Houdon, c. 1787 (American Philosophical Society). Photography by Frank Margeson.

Frontispiece. Benjamin Franklin. Oil portrait on canvas by Charles Willson Peale, copy after David Martin's 1767 portrait, 1772 (American Philosophical Society). Photography by Frank Margeson.

Fig. 1. "View of Several Public Buildings in Philadelphia," from *Columbian Magazine* 1790. From left Episcopal Academy, Congress Hall, Independence Hall, Philosophical Hall, Library Company of Philadelphia, and in background Carpenter's Hall.

Fig. 2. Thomas Jefferson. Oil portrait on canvas by Thomas Sully, 1821 (American Philosophical Society). Photography by Frank Margeson.

Fig. 3. John Vaughan. Oil portrait on canvas by Thomas Sully, 1823. (American Philosophical Society). Photography by Frank Margeson.

Fig. 4. Alexander Dallas Bache. Oil portrait on canvas by Daniel Huntington, 1861. (American Philosophical Society). Photography by Frank Margeson.

Fig. 5. Meeting Room. South side of second floor of Philosophical Hall. View looking southeast. From American Philosophical Society, *Proceedings* 22 (1885).

Fig. 6. Meeting Room. South side of second floor Philosophical Hall. View looking northwest. From American Philosophical Society, *Proceedings* 22 (1885).

Fig. 7. Frederick Fraley. Oil portrait on canvas by Margaret Lesley Bush-Brown, c. 1898 (American Philosophical Society).

Fig. 8. Philosophical Hall with 1890 third story Library addition before renovation of 1949.

Fig. 9. Interior view of 1890 third story Library addition of Philosophical Hall.

Fig. 10. Meeting Room decorated for Sesquicentennial Celebration of 1893. View looking southwest. From American Philosophical Society, *Proceedings* 32 (1893).

Fig. 11. Edward Grant Conklin. Oil portrait on canvas by Cameron Burnside, 1941 (American Philosophical Society).

Fig. 12. April 1942 Annual General Meeting. Group outside of west facade of Philosophical Hall. Seated center from left: W.F.G. Swan, Secretary; Roland S. Morris, President; Edwin G. Conklin, President-elect and Executive Officer; Luther P. Eisenhart, Executive Officer-elect.

Fig. 13. Philosophical Hall after renovation of 1949.

Fig. 14. Library Hall, 1985. Photography by Frank Margeson.

Fig. 15. Benjamin Franklin Hall, 1984. Photography by Frank Margeson.

Fig. 16. April 1986 American Philosophical Society-Royal Society Joint Meeting. View looking south at luncheon tent in Jefferson Garden with Library Hall behind. Photography by Frank Margeson.

Fig. 17. Executive Officer Herman H. Goldstine welcoming members and guests at luncheon during American Philosophical Society-Royal Society Joint Meeting.

Fig. 18. President Eliot Stellar and Librarian Edward C. Carter II in Library Reading Room thanking the Friends of the Library for their generous annual support at a recent November Friends Reception. Photography by Frank Margeson.

Preface

When I commenced this project, my initial intention was to create a souvenir for the 250th Anniversary Celebration by slightly expanding the seven-page "Brief History" which occasionally appears in the *Year Book* and fleshing it out with a few illustrations. As you can see that "modest proposal" was abandoned once I seriously began to review published sources on the American Philosophical Society's history. As this is a popular account, I have made a determined effort to limit the use of notes. A member's election date is identified when he or she is first mentioned in the text and not thereafter. Although the word "scientist" was a creation of the 1830s, I have employed the term throughout this essay when identifying men and women who worked in what are called today the mathematical, physical or biological sciences. Similarly "scholar" refers to those who pursued subjects in the social sciences or the humanities. I had hoped to discuss the Society's fine arts collection and how the cabinet of curiosities changed over the years from a museum to an art gallery, but was forced to shelve this idea due to a combination of poor planning on my part and the press of publication deadlines.

I would like to acknowledge the invaluable assistance received from the Library's 1992 seminar Mellon Interns Cynthia Dickinson, a graduate student in English at the University of North Carolina-Chapel Hill, and Robert Jackman, a graduate student in American history at the University of Kentucky, who researched and produced an excellent, detailed chronology of the Society's history for my use. I have drawn heavily on this chronology not only for detailed factual information but also its highly informative text. Also, I am indebted greatly to Julia A. Noonan for sharing her recollections with me of her long association with the Society which commenced in November 1926. Naturally, this history makes use of unsigned publications written over the years by many hands which may be considered the common property of the Society. The discussion of the Society's modern core activities is based on grant application materials prepared by John Callahan, our Development Officer, with my assistance. I would like to express my appreciation for his support of this work. Two long-time colleagues — John C. Van Horne of The Library Company of Philadelphia and Jeffrey A. Cohen of *The Papers of Benjamin Henry Latrobe* — have read the manuscript at various stages and offered specific, useful stylistic and factual criticism. As always they merit my warmest thanks.

My greatest debt, however, is to the scholar who knows the most about the American Philosophical Society's long history and numerous traditions — Whitfield J. Bell, Jr. Although personally deeply engaged in seeing his magisterial first volume of the biographical directory of the Society's early members through the press, Whit Bell made numerous useful suggestions concerning my efforts, caught egregious errors, and burnished the entire manuscript by thoughtful copy-editing. Thanks also are due to the Library staff who cheerfully responded to my many bibliographical and research queries, and, who on more than one occasion tactfully supplied me with additional photocopies of articles I had mislaid. Sandra Duffy, Secretary to the Librarian, skillfully typed various drafts of the manuscript, and Frank Margeson, the Society's Photographer, provided handsome illustrations, a number of which tested his technical virtuosity. Finally, I would like to express my deep gratitude to Herman H. Goldstine, Editor, and Carole N. Le Faivre, Associate Editor, not only for their encouragement and patience but for producing this handsome publication once the manuscript was finally delivered into their hands.

ECC II

Some General
Observations

The American Philosophical Society of Philadelphia will celebrate in April 1993 the 250th anniversary of its founding by Benjamin Franklin on May 25, 1743 and the birth of its third president, Thomas Jefferson on April 13 of the same year. These momentous events of the Society's history will be marked by four days of festivities and scholarly meetings featuring symposia on the future directions of the sciences, social sciences, and the humanities; addresses by national leaders; a concert by the Philadelphia Orchestra; and the dedication of a 400-seat auditorium, reception and catering facilities, and a state-of-the-art 120,000 volume stack floor that completes its third building — Benjamin Franklin Hall. This brief historical sketch of the American Philosophical Society's quarter of a millennium is intended to serve as a keepsake or memento of this grand occasion. It is hoped that the celebration itself will encourage a scholar to produce a much needed, full-scale history of the Society and its contributions to the world of science and learning and the culture of the United States.

In 1993, the American Philosophical Society is composed of some 570 residents and 120 foreign members of great distinction drawn from the sciences, social sciences, humanities, and public affairs. It is housed in three handsomely appointed and well-equipped buildings — Philosophical Hall (1789), Library Hall (1959), and Benjamin Franklin Hall (1984). With its endowment approaching $60 million, the American Philosophical Society carries out its mission of promoting useful knowledge by supporting scholarship through meetings, research grants,

1

publications, and its research Library.

Today the American Philosophical Society is the oldest learned society in the United States and one of the most prestigious organizations of its kind in the world. Accounts such as this often sound with a self-congratulatory ring, but perhaps on this occasion we can be forgiven for an excess of pride. To celebrate an institution's 250th anniversary is an extraordinary achievement; the story of the American Philosophical Society and those men and women members who have helped promote useful knowledge throughout the years is also extraordinary. The following general observations on these achievements and events are intended to serve as an introduction to this account of the American Philosophical Society.

The quality of membership has been uniformly high since January 1769 when the old Philosophical Society and another similar society united to create the American Philosophical Society, held at Philadelphia, for Promoting Useful Knowledge. The membership of the two societies at the time of union totaled 244 resident and twenty-one foreign members. By 1800, an additional 150 distinguished foreign scientists, scholars, and statesmen had become members. Foreign members were not merely ornamental; many donated important collections of individual books, manuscripts, and maps which today are treasures of the Library's holdings. Since 1769 the number of resident members has increased only two-and-a-third times while the general population of the nation has expanded approximately over one-hundred fold.

By April 1843, the total membership was 347, of whom 110 were foreign members and 237 resident members, half being Philadelphians. This distribution pattern continued throughout the century until 1902, when with the institution of the April Annual General Meeting, the American Philosophical Society began to transform itself once again into a more national organization. Modern authorities have argued that by the time of the Civil War the high proportion of Philadelphia members was a sign of growing provincialism and even clubbiness. Indeed the summary report of the Centennial Anniversary meeting in 1743 pointed out that "many of the leading scientific men in different sections of our country are not enrolled among our members;..." and that many members "were forcibly struck with the change which has gradually grown up in our lists, from names embracing the talent and influence of the different parts of our own Commonwealth and of the United States, to those included in more restricted and local influences" (*Proceedings*, 3 [May 1843]:216). Of course, while Philadelphia by 1850 was no longer the center of American science it was the nation's second metropolis and a great scientific, technological, publishing and industrial center capable of providing highly qualified candidates. On balance, the American Philosophical Society did elect the leading scientific figures in Philadelphia and throughout the United States, Europe, and Latin America while also adding Philadelphia doctors, lawyers, businessmen, and other amateur scientists to its rolls.

Throughout the American Philosophical Society's long history men and women of its leadership have attempted to redefine its purposes and goals, responding to needs and opportunities as they arose. Plans that had to be postponed because of inadequate financial resources reemerged in better times. The debate concerning the Society's future direction engendered by the Richard A.F. Penrose, Jr. (APS 1905) bequest of 1931 was thus not only a highly visible example of a long-standing tradition, but also profited directly from earlier ideas and proposals. In the area of financial development, the American Philosophical Society benefitted from earlier experiences. This is true of the Society's three major fund-raising efforts. In 1911 the Society decided to move to a new, modern home on Benjamin Franklin Parkway. During the late 1920s nearly half of the cost to construct and endow this facility was raised or pledged before the Great Depression checked progress and, as some would claim, better judgment dictated that the American Philosophical Society would remain in its original historical Hall. Later a significant portion of these funds together with accumulated income from another bequest paid for Library Hall, erected in 1959, which stands by authority of an act of Congress on a site within Independence National Historical Park. Library Hall is the most visible result of the Society's efforts since the early 1940s to promote the preservation and thoughtful development of the historic area. In 1981, anticipating future needs, the Society purchased and renovated the former Farmers' and Mechanics' Bank (built 1853-55) at 427 Chestnut Street, less than a block from the Hall and Library. The front third of this structure was completely rebuilt as a modern stack facility with a capacity of 300,000 volumes and two exhibition rooms; a modern air quality control system was installed and the balance of the structure prepared for future development, all at a cost of slightly more than $5 million donated by members, friends, foundations, corporations, and a federal agency. The Bank Building or Library Annex (which became operational in October 1984) was formally named in memory of Benjamin Franklin in 1987. Shortly thereafter the Benjamin Franklin Hall Campaign dedicated to the construction of a much-needed auditorium, endowment of its operation, and the completion of additional library facilities in this Hall was launched. The most ambitious and successful of the American Philosophical Society's fund-raising efforts exceeded its goal of $7 million in July 1992 by $355,000, thus guaranteeing that the renovation would be completed well in advance of the 250th Anniversary Celebration in April 1993.

This happy financial state of affairs, in fact, has only developed during the last fifth of our history. Like all individuals and institutions, the American Philosophical Society has had its ups and downs. When celebrating its 100th anniversary in May 1843 with a meeting of eight sessions at which forty-five papers were read (several of which have been hailed as classics of American science), it was not at all clear that a similar gathering would ever again be held. Earlier faced with an ever-increasing, valuable library housed in a non-fireproof building with inadequate meeting space for its membership because of income producing leases, the American Philosophical Society entered into negotiations to sell Philosophical Hall to the City of Philadelphia during the depression that followed the Panic of 1837. Before negotiations were completed the Chinese Museum building on Ninth Street was purchased with a mortgage secured by the Society's Library, paintings, and cabinet. The deal with the city fell through, the mortgage could not be paid off, and the sheriff initiated foreclosure proceedings on behalf of the creditors. At the Society's Centennial, Robert M. Patterson's (APS 1809) discussion on the institution's history concluded with a query:

> How is this to end? What account is our future historian to give of it? It will be such — we dare not doubt that it will be such — as is worthy of the Society, and of the community in which it is placed (*Proceedings*, 3 [May 1843]:36).

The members loyally came to the rescue. The obligations were met, the debts paid, and the Hall and Library saved.

The crisis of 1843 was not an isolated event, but rather symptomatic of an endemic condition. The finances of the American Philosophical Society were always rather precarious until the 1890s and then tight until 1931 when the handsome and indeed unprecedented bequest of nearly $4 million from Penrose allowed the Society to evolve into its modern configuration. Until the Society received income from the bequest, all activities had been supported by initiation fees, annual dues, rents from various tenants in the Hall, small book endowments, and a building fund. As Philadelphia's business center moved west at the beginning of this century, the income from the Hall rentals declined drastically. As late as the 1920s the Library occasionally sold duplicates and books not germane to its collections to guarantee that the Society's publications would appear regularly.

The American Philosophical Society's role in the nation's intellectual and technological evolution can only be hinted at. A reviewer of a recent study of the French Academy of Sciences stated that "even the most rigorous history of a single institution can cut no more than a thin section through a nation's scientific life." A greater claim can be made for the American Philosophical Society, especially during its early years when, as Thomas Jefferson said, it represented the best that American science had to offer the world. Led by two of the United States' most illustrious statesmen and politicians, Franklin and Jefferson — one, America's first great scientist; the other, its leading promoter of science — the American Philosophical Society's purpose and future were very much intertwined with those of the new nation. While the philosophers believed deeply in the universality of science and desired European approbation of their own scientific efforts, a strong strain of nationalism ran through their public pronouncements and private correspondence. Jefferson's *Notes on the State of Virginia*, first published in Paris 1785 — five years after his election to the Society — makes the case for republican science promoting human progress by developing America's natural and human resources. This patriotic theme resonated in the program of the American Philosophical Society and indeed throughout the nation's scientific community until the United States produced scientific works equal to those of Europe.

The American Philosophical Society considered itself a scientific society and was perceived as such by the public well into the twentieth century. While the terms "learned" and "scientific" society seem to have been employed inter-changeably, the latter was the prevalent one. The predominantly scientific nature of the organization was reflected in its membership, papers read, publications, prizes awarded, and support of activities such as the Lewis and Clark Expedition. The American Philosophical Society during its early history restricted its fields to observational and experimental science and related technologies. When elected, members joined one of six committees or sections defined in the 1769 Laws:

1. Geography, Mathematics, Natural Philosophy and Astronomy.
2. Medicine and Anatomy.

6

3. Natural History and Chemistry.
4. Trade and Commerce.
5. Mechanics and Architecture.
6. Husbandry and American Improvements.

A seventh Committee — on History, Moral Science, and General Literature — was added to the original six in 1815, thus including what are now called the "social sciences" and "humanities." By the 1920s other non-scientific fields (especially history) were playing a larger role in the society's activities and planning, and in 1936 the membership was reorganized into four Classes:

       I. Mathematical and Physical Sciences
      II. Geological and Biological Sciences
      III. Social Sciences
      IV. Humanities

Later Class II was re-classified as Biological Sciences and in April 1976, Class V — The Arts, Learned Professions and Public Affairs — was added so as to recognize men and women of multiple accomplishments and broad interests in the Jeffersonian tradition. Today the American Philosophical Society, a distinguished multi-disciplinary learned society, continues, however, to be best known for its scientific components.

The form and frequency of meetings have also changed over the years. From 1769 until 1902 stated meetings were held each month on the first and third Friday evenings except during the summer months when they were held on the third Friday. Officers were chosen in January; members were elected at first monthly, and later four times a year. In April 1902 the first Annual General Meeting was inaugurated; stated meetings continued until 1911 when they were replaced by monthly meetings. Attendance, which had dwindled at the stated meetings, then also began to decline at the monthly meetings. These meetings were replaced in November 1936 with an Autumn General Meeting. This marked the final transition of the American Philosophical Society from a Philadelphia institution to a national and international one.

For much of the Society's history the stated meetings which had an average attendance of twenty were devoted to procedural matters (finances, acknowledgment of gifts and exchanges to the Library, communications with other learned bodies and elections). The balance of these meetings was similar to modern disciplinary seminars: papers were read, discussed, and often a committee appointed to consider publication. The antecedents for the modern General Meetings are not be found in these stated meetings, but in celebratory anniversary meetings such as the Society's 1843 Centennial, the 1880 Centennial of Incorporation, the 1893 Sesquicentennial, and the famed 1906 Bicentennial of Benjamin Franklin's birth, which in many respects is the inspiration and model for the current 250th Anniversary Meeting.

If the public was asked what word best characterized the American Philosophical Society, the response might be "famous," "ancient," or "prestigious." Members closely associated with the workings of the organization might well respond with "service" or "affection." Each year members contribute thousands of committee hours judging grant applications and the quality of article and book manuscripts, planning future meetings, overseeing finances, raising needed funds, and providing counsel on Library matters. Distinguished senior scholars evaluate and debate $3,000 grants-in-aid as thoroughly and vigorously as if they were considering applications for major awards by the National Science Foundation or National Endowment for the Humanities. All these dedicated labors basically have one common purpose — to provide younger scholars with the financial and research resources and appropriate avenues of publication necessary to advance both useful knowledge and their professional careers. Rewards afforded members of the American Philosophical Society are new friendships formed in committee meetings, and old ones renewed during Annual General Meetings and Autumn General Meetings. On these occasions, it is not unusual to see lively groups of members and their spouses united not by disciplinary interests or current university affiliations, but by friendships forged decades earlier when they were beginning instructors or assistant professors on a common campus. George Gaylord Simpson (APS 1936) once wrote to a friend that he and his wife were off to Philadelphia to his favorite meeting at his favorite learned society. His affection for the American Philosophical Society has been shared by many of its members over the years. This combination of institutional service and affection help to explain in part why, now mid-way through its third century, its form and flavor remarkably little changed, the American Philosophical Society is engaged in promoting useful knowledge, as it always has been.

Creating the Society, 1743-1790

The Society's "Brief History" which is printed periodically in the *Year Book* traces the organization's early, complex evolution with admirable clarity and economy. Its language and insights combine to provide a unique vantage point from which to commence a survey of the Society's history:

"The origins of the American Philosophical Society, like those of most institutions, antedate its founding. For some years during the second quarter of the eighteenth century Philadelphians like James Logan and Joseph Breintnall had corresponded with the Royal Society of London, to which nineteen Americans were elected before 1743. They and practical men of affairs were also acquainted with the purposes and work of the Dublin Philosophical Society, founded in 1731 'for improving Husbandry, Manufactures, and other useful Arts.' In 1739 John Bartram, a Philadelphia Quaker farmer with a taste for natural history who was a correspondent of several English and Continental botanists, proposed that a society or academy of the 'most ingenious and curious men' be established in America to promote inquiries into 'natural secrets, arts & syances.' It should have a house of its own, sponsor lectures, and underwrite expeditions. The plan was, of course, too ambitious for the colonies, as Bartram's friends quickly told him. But four years later, in 1743, Benjamin Franklin took up Bartram's idea, revised and simplified it, and offered his fellow Americans 'A Proposal for Promoting Useful Knowledge among the British Plantations in America.'

The first Drudgery of Settling new Colonies, which confines the Attention of People to mere Necessaries, is now pretty well over; and there are many in every Province in Circumstances that set them at Ease, and afford Leisure to cultivate the finer Arts, and improve the common Stock of Knowledge. To such of these who are Men of Speculation, any Hints must from time to time arise, many Observations occur, which if well-examined, pursued and improved, might produce Discoveries to the Advantage of some or all of the British Plantations, or to the Benefit of Mankind in general.

But as from the Extent of the Country, such Persons are widely separated, and seldom can see and converse, or be acquainted with each other, so that many useful Particulars remain uncommunicated, die with the Discoverers, and are lost to Mankind; it is, to remedy this Inconvenience for the future, proposed.

That One Society be formed of Virtuosi or ingenious Men residing in the several Colonies, to be called the American Philosophical Society; who are to maintain a constant Correspondence. That Philadelphia being the City nearest the Centre of the Continent-Colonies, communicating with all of them northward and southward by Post, and with all the Islands by Sea, and having the Advantage of a good growing Library, be the Centre of the Society.

***

That the Subjects of the Correspondence be, all new-discovered Plants, Herbs, Trees, Roots, &c. Methods of Propagating them, and making such as are useful, but particular to some Plantations, more general. Improvements of vegetable Juices, as Cyders, Wines &c. New Methods of Curing or Preventing Diseases. All new-discovered Fossils in different Countries, as Mines, Minerals, Quarries, &c. New and useful Improvements in Distillation, Brewing,

12

Assaying of Ores, &c. New mechanical Inventions for Saving Labour; as Mills, Carriages, &c. and for Raising and Conveying of Water, Draining of Meadows, &c. All new Arts, Trades, Manufactures, &c. that may be proposed or thought of. Surveys, Maps and Charts of particular Parts of the Sea-coasts, or Inland Countries; Course and Junction of Rivers and great Roads, Situation of Lakes and Mountains, Nature of the Soil and Productions, &c. New Methods of Improving the Breed of useful Animals, Introducing other Sorts from foreign Countries. New Improvements in Planting, Gardening, Clearing Land, &c. And all philosophical Experiments that let Light into the Nature of Things, tend to increase the Power of Man over Matter, and multiply the Conveniences or Pleasure of Life.

"The American Philosophical Society was organized on this plan in early 1744. It held several meetings, elected to membership such men as the naturalists Dr. John Clayton and Dr. John Mitchell of Virginia, and the mathematicians James Alexander and Cadwallader Colden of New York, and received learned papers, which Franklin planned to publish in an American philosophical miscellany. But interest soon lagged — the Philadelphia members, on whom success depended, Franklin complained, 'are very idle Gentlemen; they will take no Pains' — and by 1746 the Society was moribund, if not dead.

"Twenty year later, in the wake of American resistance to the Stamp Act, another society was formed. Calling itself the American Society for Promoting Useful Knowledge, it was composed of younger Philadelphians, generally anti-proprietary in politics, champions of American rights, who were determined to strengthen the colonies economically as well as politically. Charles Thomson, later secretary of the Continental Congress, spelled out its program: improved methods of farming, including the breeding of livestock, new medicines and cures for specific diseases, new manufactures and improvements in the old, new sources of mineral wealth. 'But it is not proposed,' he added, 'to confine the view of the Society, wholly, to these things, so as to exclude other useful subjects, either in physics, mechanics, astronomy, mathematics, &c.' The Society proved astonishingly successful. But older men, including survivors of the 1743 group, many of whom were members of the Proprietary Party, taking umbrage that they had not been invited to join, revived the American Philosophical Society, which they claimed had only been 'dormant.' In 1768, therefore, there were two societies of similar purpose, organization, and scope, though distinguished by the political and religious views of their Philadelphia members. Both were intercolonial and even international in membership. Good sense and good will eventually prevailed, and on 2 January 1769, the two societies were merged as 'The American Philosophical Society, held at Philadelphia, for Promoting Useful Knowledge.' Franklin, who was then a colonial agent in England, was chosen President.

"In its work the new society reflected both the spirit of the Royal Society, its prototype, and the practical concerns of the original American Society for Promoting Useful Knowledge and its model, the Society of Arts and Manufacturers of London. It conducted observations of the transit of Venus in 1769, which, published in the Royal Society's *Philosophical Transactions*, at once established the Philadelphia society's international reputation. These observations were also reported in the Society's own *Transactions*, of which the first volume appeared in 1771. Copies were sent to the learned academies of Europe, which responded with copies of their own publications: and thus were established exchanges which continue to the present day" (1990 *Year Book*, 351-53). The American Philosophical Society also established a committee to survey possible canal routes across the Delmarva Peninsula linking the Chesapeake Bay to the Delaware River so as to bring the trade of Maryland into the port of Philadelphia. The committee's abridged report and a map of the routes were published in the first volumes of the *Transactions*. The survey books were to prove useful both to the English-trained architect and engineer Benjamin Henry Latrobe's (APS 1799) uncompleted Chesapeake and Delaware

Canal project of 1804-06 and later to William Strickland (APS 1820), who executed the initial survey of the canal's main line in the early 1820s.

The American Revolution struck a heavy blow at the Society, as it did to most of the new states' institutions. Political feelings could no longer be put aside; Loyalists and Quaker pacifists soon ceased entirely from attendance; the Library and Museum were scattered; meetings were given up. Neither the election of a constellation of military heroes nor incorporation by the Pennsylvania legislature in 1780 stimulated the body into renewed vigor. In 1782 the Society was described by one of its members as "in a very languishing state."

The return of Benjamin Franklin in September 1785 from Paris, where since December 1776 he had served as United States Minister to the French Court and later helped negotiate the 1783 Treaty of Peace with Great Britain, materially reinvigorated the American Philosophical Society. His reputation and popularity were immense; scientists and savants throughout Europe for years had sent Franklin their publications, which he in turn forwarded to Philadelphia for the Society's Library. At a meeting on September 18, 1785, he strengthened the members' resolve to build Philosophical Hall by cleverly presenting two exciting scientific papers for discussion — thus reasserting the Society's scientific roots and purposes — before presenting the actual motion to approve the construction project. Later Franklin generously supported the enterprise with a major contribution and loan.

The rest of the decade saw a vigorous renewal of activity. A second volume of *Transactions* was issued in 1786, and a bequest of £200 was received to establish the first of the Society's prizes. The permanent home of its own required for the American Philosophical Society to sustain this momentum, create viable long-term research and publication programs, and flourish generally over the years, became a reality. The Society had met in various buildings: the College of Philadelphia (later the University of Pennsylvania), the Christ Church Schoolhouse,

Carpenters' Hall, and, on occasion, the homes of officers. "A portion of the State House Yard was deeded to the Society in 1785, and there Philosophical Hall was constructed in 1785-89. The persons principally responsible for this reawakening were Francis Hopkinson (APS 1769), a state official and signer of the Declaration of Independence, and Samuel Vaughan (APS 1784), an English Whig and friend of America, now a resident of Philadelphia. Vaughan's son John (APS 1784) was to remain in Philadelphia, where he became treasurer of the Society in 1791 and librarian in 1803, holding both posts until his death in 1841" (1990 *Year Book*, 353).

The first stated meeting of the Society in its own Hall occurred on Friday, November 20, 1789. With this event, the first stage of the journey commenced in 1743 with the publication of Benjamin Franklin's "Proposal" was successfully completed.

Fig. 1. "View of Several Public Buildings in Philadelphia," from *Columbian Magazine* 1790. From left Episcopal Academy, Congress Hall, Independence Hall, Philosophical Hall, Library Company of Philadelphia, and in background Carpenters' Hall.

17

The New Nation's Scientific Society, 1790-1848

For nearly half a century, the American Philosophical Society was the leader of all science in the young Republic — no other scientific institution demonstrated its consistency, nor had its constellation of great men. The nation's second scientific organization the American Academy of Action Sciences of Boston, founded in 1780 by John Adams (APS 1780) who was inspired by the example of the Society and impressed by its European prestige, carried on a broad range of valuable activities while remaining essentially a Massachusetts institution. Benjamin Silliman (APS 1805), the Yale chemist and geologist, established the *American Journal of Science* in 1818 which for the next two decades was perceived both in the United States and Europe to be America's best known and most highly respected scientific journal. With the establishment of the American Association for the Advancement of Science in 1848 and the rise of federal science in Washington, D.C. the Society's reputation declined relatively somewhat and it was perceived by some to be essentially a regional organization serving the rapidly growing Philadelphia metropolis.

"As the principal learned society in the United States, the Society in those early years of the republic often served as a national library, museum, and academy of sciences. Thomas Jefferson, who was president of the United States and of the Society simultaneously, called on it for advice: at his request, for example, the Society prepared what were in effect the scientific instructions for Lewis and Clark, and Jefferson deposited the report of their expedition in the Society's library, where it remains. Other officers and departments of government called on the Society for the loan of maps, telescopes, and other scientific apparatus; while John Quincy Adams borrowed from the Society a crate of books on weights and measures, which he consulted at Quincy during the summer he composed his great report on the subject.

"Accepting the presidency of the Society in 1797, Jefferson asserted that the Society 'comprehends whatever the American World has of distinction in Philosophy & Science in general.' So it must have seemed. The members felt their obligation to promote American science and learning in all possible ways. They offered a premium for the plan of education best calculated to promote the welfare of a republic, and another on whether it was 'the duty and interest of the Community, to provide for the Education of Youth.' At the same time they continued to encourage discoveries in new and applied science -- ships' pumps, stoves and fireplaces, peach blight, vegetable dyes, street lighting. And Jefferson and others placed in the library hundreds of word-lists and other materials that recorded and illustrated the life, customs, and languages of the Indian inhabitants of America" (1990 *Year Book*, 354).

During much of this time the "Hall" of the American Philosophical Society consisted of the second floor southwest corner room of Philosophical Hall, the rest of the building being leased to various tenants. In 1789, the University of Pennsylvania secured a five-year lease for the greater part of the building. Upon the expiration of the university's lease, the rent was raised and a more "desirable tenant," Charles Willson Peale (APS 1786), the famed artist, moved in his large family and his museum for the next fifteen years. The remarkable Charles Willson Peale -- artist, investor, educator, and museum keeper was a close friend of Thomas Jefferson and a member of his intellectual and political circle. Thus from 1794 to 1811 Philosophical Hall housed America's earliest successful museum.

Fig. 2. Thomas Jefferson. Oil portrait on canvas by Thomas Sully, 1821 (American Philosophical Society). Photography by Frank Margeson.

When the museum expanded beyond its capacity, the Long Room and additional space in the State House were leased in 1802 to accommodate the Peales' numerous portraits of American heroes and other worthies and the constantly increasing natural history specimens and menagerie of native animals. Two of

21

Peale's sons were born in the Hall — one appropriately named Franklin.

These were indeed lively, stimulating, and on occasion frightening times for the Hall and the Society's membership. Philadelphia was the nation's capital during the decade of the 1790s. The horrors of the 1793 yellow fever epidemic were made real when the Fellows of the College of Physicians met in the Hall at the request of the mayor to mobilize the city's medical resources in an attempt to cope with the plague which would claim the lives of Society members and their families. Later the city witnessed the outbreak of political conflict and strife as the Federalists and Jeffersonian Republicans fought for control of the national government. Jefferson triumphed in the presidential election of 1800, but not before he was ridiculed for his membership in and leadership of "a club of illiterate Jacobins," a subversive pack of atheists and idealists who aimed at overthrowing good Federalist social order. Evidently, however, in the Hall itself Federalists and Republicans conducted the Society's business without rancor, avoiding religion and politics.

Thomas Sully, the well-known portrait painter, maintained his studio and gallery in Philosophical Hall from 1812 to 1822. John Vaughan, one of the Society's greatest servants, who in 1787 had rented the cellar for the storage of wines and liquors of his importing business, established bachelor apartments in the Hall when the Peales moved out. John Vaughan as Librarian, collected political and economic pamphlets and books with both hands, forged close ties with European scholars and institutions, especially those interested in Native American linguistics and ethnohistory, and in 1839 proposed that a great national library and union catalogue be established in Washington with the Smithson bequest. Cheerful, extremely knowledgeable about Philadelphia, he was the city's cicerone to countless visitors who first enjoyed Vaughan's sumptuous breakfasts before commencing sightseeing. Respected and beloved by many, John Vaughan lived out his life in Philosophical Hall and upon his death in 1841 lay in state there. This honor was also later accorded Alexander Dallas Bache (APS 1829), a great-grandson of Franklin and the first president of the National Academy of Sciences, and also to a lesser degree Dr. Judson Daland (1860-1937), a benefactor of the Society, whose ashes are interred in a wall of the Hall.

The death in 1818 of another esteemed member, Dr. Caspar Wistar (APS 1787), professor of anatomy at the University

Fig. 3. John Vaughan. Oil portrait on canvas by Thomas Sully, 1823. (American Philosophical Society). Photography by Frank Margeson.

of Pennsylvania, resulted in the establishment of a famous Philadelphia institution and a social adjunct of the American Philosophical Society — the Wistar Association or Wistar Party. In 1799 or 1800, Dr. Wistar began holding small receptions at his home on Sunday evenings for "strangers" — interesting visitors to the city, a core group of philosopher friends, and a few other Philadelphians. Conversation was the centerpiece of these evenings with a heavy emphasis on scientific and medical topics. The food and drink, while enjoyable, was modest. The high quality of the conversation is recorded in memoirs and travelers' accounts. When Dr. Wistar died, his Society friends mourned his passing, along with the demise of his Wistar Parties. The following fall the tradition was continued when the Wistar Association was established by eight of his local American Philosophical Society friends; by 1821 the number had increased to sixteen and seven years later it reached twenty-four. Each member was required to host two receptions annually at his home during the non-summer months. A few historians such as Simon Baatz have claimed that the Wistar Party also constituted a powerful secret inner group — a cabal — which attempted to influence the development of Philadelphia science by supporting the efforts of some individuals and institutions while placing obstacles in the progress of others. Although Alexander Dallas Bache (APS 1829) was a member of the Wistar Association, it is difficult to conceive of it as a local precedent for the "Lazzaroni," the "nucleus of a half-dozen or so scientific organizers and policymakers" that Bache as superintendent of the United States Coast Survey and Joseph Henry (APS 1835), as secretary of the Smithsonian Institution, gathered to "shape a vision of what American science should be" (Bruce, *Launching Science*, 18). The sole purpose of the Wistar Party was to give a good party with excellent conversation — a principle that is honored today by its current membership.

Whenever possible the American Philosophical Society actively fostered the scientific relationship that had been established with the federal government during the Lewis and

Clark expedition. When Major Stephen H. Long (APS 1823) led his 1819 Expedition to the Rocky Mountains, the Society at the request of the Secretary of War suggested subjects for scientific investigation and nominated people to accompany the party. Long thanked the Society, and with official approval sent a collection of plants to Philadelphia. Later a number of the Long Expedition's scientists' reports were published in the *Transactions*. The Society performed a similar service in the planning of the United States Exploring Expedition of 1838-1842, or South Seas Expedition as it was then commonly called. Commanded by Lieutenant Charles Wilkes (APS 1843), the expedition comprised six naval vessels with some five hundred officers, crew, scientists, and artists aboard and gave a good account of itself. It enhanced the reputation of American science worldwide by charting some two hundred islands, mostly in the Pacific, discovering the Antarctic Continent, and bringing home natural history collections of unprecedented proportions that helped develop the first great federal institutions of science — The United States Botanic Garden, The National Herbarium, The Naval Observatory, and The National Museum (*Bell*, "APS as NAS," 171). Today one of the prized possessions of the Society's Library are Titian Ramsay Peale's beautiful watercolors and sketches that document brilliantly both this great enterprise and the Long Expedition.

America's leading scientists such as the chemist Robert Hare (APS 1803; inventor of the oxy-hydrogen blow pipe and a pioneer in the study of the constitution of salts), Joseph Henry, and Alexander Dallas Bache presented papers and conducted experimental demonstrations in Philosophical Hall until the mid 1840s. Henry, the nation's greatest physical scientist whose path-breaking work on electromagnetism was universally applauded made it a regular practice to consult scientific journals not available to him at Princeton. Working in Philosophical Hall at what came to be known as "Mr. Henry's desk" he gathered and analyzed information and data that, combined with his own laboratory research, resulted in articles that were published in the

Proceedings. Alexander Dallas Bache, a geophysicist famed for his research on terrestrial magnetism, was an officer of the American Philosophical Society for twenty-five years, being Secretary from 1832 to 1844, Vice-President 1845-1854 and President 1855-1857. Although he lacked his friend Henry's rare analytical and theoretical skills, Bache was a brilliant scientific manager and promoter, whose consuming professional goal was to make American science equal to that of Europe. Following an early career at the University of Pennsylvania, Bache was elected president of Girard College in 1836, spent three years in Europe investigating educational institutions for the Girard College trustees, became president of Central High School and superintendent of the Philadelphia public school system, which he reorganized, and then returned to his professorship of natural philosophy and chemistry at Pennsylvania. In December 1843, he was made head of the Coast Survey in Washington, D.C., a position from which he helped shape federal science policy and operations until his death in 1867. Bache, the only professional scientist among the Smithsonian's regents, skillfully prepared the way for Henry to become the institution's first head (somewhat against the Princetonian's initial desires).

Following the War of 1812, the American Philosophical Society accelerated. President Peter S. Du Ponceau (APS 1791) the French-born lawyer who together with Thomas Jefferson and Albert Gallatin (APS 1791) made the Society the center of Native American linguistics and ethnohistory, presented a wry, verbal program report on publications in December 1836. He noted that with the appearance of volume six of the *Transactions* in 1809 "we went to sleep for nine years" but "in the year 1818, we awoke & published the first Volume of a new series of our *Transactions*." These volumes now began to appear more regularly in a larger format. By the time of Du Ponceau's report, the Society had published four volumes of the new *Transactions* and had one in press. It also issued two volumes of the Historical and Literary Committee *Transactions* dedicated to linguistics studies and in 1824 the Library's first printed catalogue. Du Ponceau

Fig. 4. Alexander Dallas Bache. Oil portrait on canvas by Daniel
Huntington, 1861. (American Philosophical Society).
Photography by Frank Margeson.

concluded, "We are advancing and must not lose our Courage;
our best publications have followed each pretty close, and shows
that the spirit among us is not extinct." The philosophers took
this charge to heart and two years later the first volume of the

27

Society's *Proceedings (1838)* appeared; early volumes included the minutes of stated meetings and abstracts of papers presented or read at the Society's meetings. In 1886, the American Philosophical Society formally adopted a policy distinguishing between the two publications: papers exceeding twenty-four pages of the *Proceedings* format, as well as those requiring engravings on full-page plates thereafter were to be published in the *Transactions*.

The American Philosophical Society's direct participation in an international scientific project was as a part of the "Magnetic Crusade" "launched in 1837 under the direction of the British Association for the Advancement of Science, with the aid of the Royal Society and the patronage of the British government." Responding to the British appeal, the Society, acting on Alexander Dallas Bache's recommendation, "urged the Secretary of War to establish five observatories in the United States, each with the necessary instruments and personnel." The Philadelphia observatory (at Girard College) went into operation in 1839, its work was directed by Bache, and its expenses were defrayed by private contributions from the Society, its members and friends, but at the end of 1842 the observations were stopped by lack of funds. By that time, however, the observatory's work had proved to be so valuable that the War Department (strenuously lobbied by the Society) came forward with financial support; the work continued; and the reports of the entire series of observations, 472 regular observations daily, were published by order of the government" (*Bell*, "APS as NAS," 171-72). The story of the Girard College observatory does credit to the American Philosophical Society, which was able to promote the cause of terrestrial magnetism even though it did not have enough influence to generate interest in establishing the other five observatories. It demonstrated that the Society could support a financially modest scientific undertaking for only a short time. It possessed neither the organizational nor financial resources to compete on a larger scale. Thus the Society was not unlike many other intellectual and social institutions in

28

Jacksonian America that patched financial resources together to support small-scale operations.

The papers, reports, and public accounts of the American Philosophical Society's 1843 Centennial meeting show the Society's interests were broad-gauged, impressive by modern standards, and full of promise for the Society's future. Although the Society conducted its affairs under the threat of the sheriff's writ and all expenses were borne by individual members, the celebration was a quality performance as demonstrated by the prompt publication and special volume devoted to its activities (*Proceedings*, 3 [May 1843]). Deciding to mount the celebration only several months previously, the Society canvassed the American scientific community successfully for papers in all the major disciplines. This was a fitting task for America's oldest and only general scientific body. Not only was the stated purpose of that landmark gathering to review the history of the Society and present "it as the guardian of the scientific reputation of its founders" but "also to mark the present condition of science in the United States, by calling its cultivators to meetings where they might bring their latest contributions...." As many respondents to the Society's invitation had observed, it was important to assemble around the "Society the men of science of the country, for mutual encouragement, support and improvement."

The oration on the American Philosophical Society's history was delivered by Robert M. Patterson (APS 1809), Director of the United States Mint, at the Musical Fund Society Hall a few blocks from the State House yard at 8th and Locust Streets on May 25th before a large audience composed of delegates from other scientific societies, many invited guests from other parts of the country, members of different Philadelphia associations, and religious bodies, judicial and municipal authorities, officers of the army and navy stationed in Philadelphia, professors and students of the university and local colleges, and a respectable number of interested citizens. The attendance of the faculty and students of Central High School was a hopeful sign for the future development of American science. Under Alexander Dallas Bache's leadership, the High School, which was comparable to a German *gymnasium*, had surpassed the University of Pennsylvania in scientific energy and spirit in the early 1840s and boasted "the best equipped astronomical observatory in the nation, winning a European reputation with it" (Bruce, *Launching Science*, 47). The Committee of Arrangements' following observation captures the forward-looking tone of the Centennial:

> The interest of the meetings was much increased by the presence, generally, of the authors of memoirs, and by the care taken in preparing suitable diagrams and drawings for illustration. In this connection, the Committee have pleasure in referring to the kind services of certain pupils of the High School, detailed with the consent of their parents by the Principal, to assist in preparing drawings, and to attend at the meetings as aids to the Committee of Arrangement. Many of the diagrams were executed by these youths in a style which did them great credit; and to their faithful assiduity during the meetings, and at other times, the Committee were much indebted. The attendance at all the meetings of many strangers and citizens, not members of the Society, manifesting untiring attention in the proceedings, an intelligent zeal in behalf of science, and a warm interest in the success of its cultivators, was in the highest degree cheering.

The success of the celebration caused some members to consider expanded leadership roles for the American Philosophical Society that could be accomplished with modest external financial support. One idea put forward several times was that the Society should be the organizing core of a larger national general scientific body of some kind. As early as the 1780s, it had been proposed that the American Philosophical Society coordinate the activities and serve as the informational clearing house of a constellation or confederation of sister philosophical societies established in every state, but nothing resulted. In 1838 the American Academy of Arts and Science of Boston urged that both institutions join to form an American association for the promotion of science. Joseph Henry, who knew first-hand about the British Association for the Advancement of Science's inclusion of enthusiastic but often misguided amateurs, feared such a policy might retard or even destroy attempts to foster professional science in the United States. The American Philosophical Society followed Henry's advice and politely declined the Bostonians' offer as "inexpedient." This tension between elitist expertise and democratic amateurism would plague American science well beyond the founding of the National Academy of Sciences in 1863.

The momentum generated by the Society's Centennial produced nothing lasting and others decided that the time had arrived to establish a national general scientific association which, aided by railroad transportation, could hold its annual meetings in the major cities of the nation. The Association of American Geologists and Naturalists had already adopted a constitution similar to that of the British Association and at its 1847 meeting in Boston voted to transform itself into the American Association for the Advancement of Science with a far more open membership than honorific organizations such as the American Philosophical Society. At its Philadelphia meeting in September the following year, the new constitution was unanimously adopted. All of the city's major scientific organizations save the American Philosophical Society offered hospitality and/or sent friendly messages of congratulations and greetings to the new organization. This aloof, even rude behavior of the philosophers is difficult to comprehend today hinting as it does of an attitude of provincial self-satisfaction. "The Society was still the oldest but it was no longer the first, American scientific society" (Bell, "APS as NAS," 174).

The Quiet Years,
1848-1900

"After mid-century the American Philosophical Society's position in the learned world was no longer unique or preeminent. Other institutions were meeting the needs of the growing scientific community. Societies like the Academy of Natural Sciences of Philadelphia appealed to specialists; Silliman's *Journal* offered speedy publication of learned papers. Furthermore, the federal government, which originally supported no agencies for science, now created several of its own — the Coast and Geodetic Survey, the Corps of Topographical Engineers, and finally the Smithsonian Institution. The Society, on the other hand, though it recognized men of distinction throughout the country and seldom failed to elect those who might be thought to deserve election, was largely a Philadelphia institution, in the hands of local people" (the 1990 *Year Book*, 354).

The traditional characterization of the Society during these years had been as an institution continuing in its earlier pattern, without much vigor or originality. "Someone told Henry Thoreau, who spent several hours one day in 1854 happily exploring the Academy of Natural Sciences of Philadelphia, that the Society was a company of old women; and he did not bother to visit its hall" (Bell, "As Others Saw Us," 274). The geologist J. Peter Lesley (APS 1856) recalled that when he was a new member in the latter 1850s, the older members raced through the formal business meeting, offering scant comment or praise to the authors of papers, then drew their chairs around the fire to exchange gossip, jokes, and even ribald stories. Clearly things

33

have improved tremendously since J. Peter Lesley joined the Society. It certainly received some bad press during this period — some well deserved but a good deal of it not. Throughout these years not inconsiderable accomplishments were taking place and the ground was being prepared quietly for future, critical new developments in the Society's history.

The most commendable achievement of these years was the publication record of the *Transactions* and the *Proceedings*. Good work continued to be published in these journals although they "had a natural history emphasis, which meant that government publications increasingly overshadowed them" (Bruce, *Launching Science*, 243). Joseph Henry, for example, who in the 1840s had used the Society as his major publication vehicle, no longer did so by 1850. Papers on geology, paleontology, and North and Central Native American linguistics, anthropology, and archaeology replaced the physical sciences offerings. The best known and most prolific contributors were Edward D. Cope (APS 1843), who waged war with his fellow member and arch-rival Othniel Marsh (APS 1868), Joseph Leidy (APS 1849), who eschewed any conflict, Ferdinand V. Hayden (APS 1860), J. Peter Lesley (APS 1856), Daniel G. Brinton (APS 1869), and their younger colleague Franz Boas (APS 1903). Meetings became more lively in the 1890s, especially when the irascible Cope was involved. At a symposium on "Factors of Organic Evolution" during the stated meeting of May 1, 1896, Cope spoke on the subject from the paleontological standpoint. When it came to printing the papers in the *Proceedings*, Cope angrily refused because as he had previously stated, his contained no new knowledge. The Society's Secretary threatened to publish the stenographer's record of the papers whether they were revised or not, and Cope exploded and informed the Society he was consulting a lawyer. The dog fight went on for several months, when the symposium finally appeared with an explanatory footnote — "Prof. Cope being unwilling to furnish the Society with the text of his remarks, or to have the stenographic copy printed in the *Proceedings*, his part of the joint discussion must be omitted — Secretaries" (Bonner and Bell, "What is Money For," 79). Cope, whose Society publication record was unmatched, was a presence even after death. In 1907, the *Transactions* (21 Part 4) was devoted to a "Study of the Brains of Six Eminent Scientists and Scholars belonging to the American Anthropometric Society, together with a description of the skull of Professor E. D. Cope."

There were, of course, other significant achievements in the second half of the nineteenth century. The American Philosophical Society financially assisted Elisha Kent Kane (APS 1851) in his Arctic exploration in the 1850s. Ferdinand V. Hayden, the great geologist, proposed in 1867 that a photographic record of Native Americans west of the Mississippi be undertaken by "the presentation of photographs of persons and scenery from that part of the country in albums of the Society." A committee was appointed "to produce photographic portraits of North American Indians for ethnological purposes" and fifty dollars was appropriated for the purpose. Later that year Hayden undertook the first of his great western surveys. A few years later he employed the renowned William Henry Jackson to execute both geological and ethnographic photography.

Eighteen sixty-nine witnessed the election of Maria Mitchell, first woman astronomer in America; Mary Somerville, celebrated English mathematician and scientist; and Elizabeth Cady Agassiz, pioneer in women's education. These three women were the first to have been elected by the American Philosophical Society since Princess Ekatherina Romanovna Dashkova, president of the St. Petersburg Imperial Academy of Science, became the Society's first female member in 1789. *The Early Proceedings of the American Philosophical Society for the Promotion of Useful Knowledge (1744-1838)* was compiled from manuscript minutes of meetings. This 1884 publication made a record of the Society's early activities and concerns more widely and readily accessible.

The Civil War, America's most destructive and bloodiest conflict, was hardly mentioned in the American Philosophical

Fig. 5. Meeting Room. South side of second floor of Philosophical Hall. View looking southeast. From American Philosophical Society, *Proceedings* 22 (1885).

Fig. 6. Meeting Room. South side of second floor Philosophical Hall. View looking northwest. From American Philosophical Society, *Proceedings* 22 (1885).

Society's official records and publications. Meetings continued, but social occasions like those of the Wistar Party stopped meeting. As one member put it, "I find myself so distressed in the present unhappy conditions of things as to be unfit for society..."; another was against resuming parties until "the Civil War is ended ... [as] I feel quite sure that the parties would not be harmonious" because political discussions could not be prevented (*Wistar Party Sketch*, 16). Scientist members who were professional naval or military officers served in the Union forces, often with distinction. Unlike the American Revolution, when a large proportion of Washington's general staff were made members of the Society, only a few military figures, one being Rear Admiral Samuel Francis Du Pont (APS 1862), were elected during the conflict; Ulysses S. Grant was elected three years after Appomattox. Alexander Dallas Bache, who before the war had been a great admirer of Jefferson Davis because of his effective long-term support of federal science, was turned into "an uncompromising Unionist" by Secession. Bache worked tirelessly making the Coast Survey an indispensable asset to both the Navy and the Army, actively planning coastal and blockade operations, and serving as vice-president of the Sanitary Commission. His health, already threatened by overwork, was seriously impaired in 1863 when Lee threatened Pennsylvania. Responding to the mayor of Philadelphia's plea to superintend plans to protect the city, Bache worked an eighteen-hour-a-day schedule throughout that sultry summer. A year later he was forced to retire from work and died in February 1867 at sixty (Bruce, *Launching Science*, 274 and 298-99).

Five years earlier, a highly unusual, some might say the most disgraceful, event in the long history of the American Philosophical Society occurred in Philosophical Hall on March 21, 1862, when two regular United States naval officers Matthew Fontaine Maury (APS 1852) and William Francis Lynch (APS 1853), who on the secession of their native state Virginia had resigned their commissions and joined the Confederate Navy — were expelled from the American Philosophical Society for having "committed public and notorious acts of Treason against the United States." The vote was "23 ayes and 3 noes." Franklin Bache (APS 1820), the venerable former President of the Society (1853-55), a great-grandson of our founder, who as a young member in the 1820s had communicated with the great Jefferson on behalf of the Society, tried twice unsuccessfully to derail the expulsion movement. In the end, he declined to vote and was excused. The 27 members present constituted an extremely large meeting; one-third of the "ayes" had never before or rarely had attended a Society meeting.

Matthew Fontaine Maury was perhaps in the eyes of the general public the nation's best known scientific figure. Maury helped create a whole new science appropriate to the age — a "physical geography of the sea" — that came to be known as oceanography. He was the stormy petrel of antebellum science, "The Pathfinder of the Seas," and the nemesis of the leader of the American scientific establishment, Alexander Dallas Bache. The two men, who have been called the "Barons of Bureaucracy," had waged an intense political competition throughout the 1850s over federal funding for their respective agencies and definition of operational turf. The heart of Maury's scientific work that captured the imagination of the American public and the scientific authorities of European maritime nations was the *Wind and Current Charts* and *Explanations and Sailing Directions* to accompany those charts, that were issued by the Naval Observatory which Maury had headed since 1844. The value of Maury's work was immense. Using these charts captains were able to cut down their sailing time between New York and Rio de Janeiro by as much as thirty-five percent. As his work expanded to include winds and currents of other areas, ships following his charts from New York to California were able to cut more than six weeks from what had previously been the normal sailing time. William Lynch was a close friend and associate of Maury, a fact that did not recommend him to the Philadelphia philosophers. He had no real scientific reputation. His election to the Society was based on his leadership of the U.S. Expedition to the Dead Sea and the River Jordan in 1848, the account of which was published by Maury's Naval Observatory in 1852.

What is to be made of this entire affair? It is unique in the history of the Society, which had weathered other bitter political storms without resorting to the expulsion of members. It had Tory members, and non-juring Quaker members who would not swear allegiance to the state of Pennsylvania during the Revolution. During the bitterest days of party rivalry in the 1790s, Federalists and Republicans comported themselves civilly here in the Hall — leaving political strife and acrimony next door in the Chambers of Congress.

Perhaps Maury and Lynch were simply seen as traitors in a life and death struggle for the Union that was not going so well for the North. A Boston newspaper had put a $2,500 reward on Maury's head alleging that as superintendent of the Depot of Charts and Instruments he had ordered the surreptitious alteration of marker buoys at the entrance of southern harbors and that he had taken secret Southern coastal charts with him to Richmond. No modern historian mentions these charges. Alexander Dallas Bache and Joseph Henry were delighted when the "Southern Humbug" left Washington because his departure opened up the directorship of the Naval Observatory for their man, James M. Gilliss (APS 1848), the distinguished Navy astronomer, and effectively put an end to Maury's scientific efforts, thereby diminishing his reputation among the educated American public.

The conspiratorial view of history might cast March 21, 1862 in different terms. Perhaps it was not so clear that Maury was finished as a force in American science; his reputation remained high in European public circles and institutions. Perhaps the vote by Bache's Philadelphia friends and colleagues was part of an effort to make certain that Maury and his kind of old-fashioned science would not return. In 1865, Bache threw out as "worthless" all of Maury's data upon which his *Wind and Current Charts* and his *Sailing Directions* had been based. The previous year the National Academy of Sciences had passed a resolution condemning these publications as embracing "much which is unsound in philosophy and little that is practically useful...."

On April 4, 1862, two of the three members who had voted against expulsion — Frederick Fraley (APS 1842) and Eli Kirk Price (1854) — had their individual reasons for their actions "entered upon the minutes." (No mention of their objections appears in the printed version of the minutes.) Price's third and final reason affirmed the principles that the American Philosophical Society always has honored save on this one occasion:

> Because... it does not comport with the true and enduring dignity and welfare of the Society, thus to proceed against the course of the law for the removal of members, and thus for political causes to interrupt the harmony of scientific and peaceful pursuits.

If the balance of these years in Philosophical Hall was generally quiet, they were not always free of "personal rivalries and antipathies." Competition for office was present. One historian has claimed that the "Society suffered from a persistent struggle between amateurs and professionals" (Bruce, *Launching Science*, 249). Isaac Lea (APS 1828), a publisher turned productive naturalist, and long-time Dean of the Wistar Party, gave a brutal assessment of the non-scientific direction he judged the Society to have taken. In October 1858, when welcoming Samuel Powel (APS 1855) to Wistar Party membership, he bitterly described the Society's elections of the night before in which only two of four previously black-balled scientists were narrowly elected. Lea gloomily concluded:

> This is a very sad business....I do not think the Society can be saved — such has been my opinion all along. The ruling power has been building up for 15 or 20 years, and there is now nothing to enable us, who look only to the interests of science, to overcome that influence, so destructive to the objects for which the Society was originally formed by

Franklin & his friends. I feel deeply mortified to see the old Society which I once loved so much, brought to such decrepitude under the management of politicians & ignoramuses. Fortunately for the character of Philadelphia it will be saved by the labour of the Academy [of Natural Sciences]. That noble institution must be kept with a single eye to the advancement of the sciences of the country (Lea to Powel, October 16, 1858, copy APSL).

From 1857 to the end of the century, the Society's presidency was held by a lawyer-judge for one year, a distinguished professor of medicine for twenty years, and a merchant-banker for twenty-one years. If this was not the most brilliant period of leadership the American Philosophical Society has known, it was not the disaster some critics have made it out to be. It may be true that in the final two decades the Society "became increasingly a social club and a local institution as its national flavor faded" (*APS News*, June 1992, 5), but there is more to the story than that. These men and their colleagues faced difficult choices during hard times; they finished their run with a financially stronger institution that was feeling its way towards a new agenda. A key figure in this process was Frederick Fraley, whose membership spanned fifty-eight years during which time he was an officer for twenty-nine years before his presidency (1880-1901). He was an intelligent, friendly man of strong character (as exemplified by his stand against the expulsion of Maury and Lynch), devoted to the Society and its traditional scientific role, who struggled for years with the institution's complex financial and legal problems.

The United States government offered to purchase Philosophical Hall and its lot for $78,000 in 1856 as a facility for the Federal Courts. Because of the limitations in the original Pennsylvania Act of 1784 that deeded the property to the Society, the United States Attorney General refused to consummate the sale. This was the first of a series of flawed attempts to sell the Hall and move the Society to a modern, more

Fig. 7. Frederick Fraley. Oil portrait on canvas by Margaret
Lesley Bush-Brown, c. 1898 (American Philosophical Society).

centrally located site in Philadelphia. The need for a better
designed, fire-proof building to accommodate the rapidly
increasing collections of books and manuscripts, and the
portraits, instruments, historic furniture, and other Society
treasures was a subject of regular discussion. A building fund had
been established in 1866 as an independent trust to erect a fire-

proof building "for the security of the books and property of the Society." By 1890 the trust had sufficient funds to pay for the expansion and alteration of Philosophical Hall — a process that was deemed "The Folly of the Third Story" in the 1950s. A Committee on Extended Accommodations recommended that a third story be added to accommodate the Library. William E. Lingelbach, (APS 1916) a distinguished historian and the Society's Librarian, later gave this somewhat sarcastic account of the project:

> the walls had to be strengthened and iron pillars installed in the rooms on the first and second floors to carry the extra load. The entire improvements including the new book cases in the large upper library room cost the sum of $41,449.72.
>
> The costly addition of the "dungeon-like" superstructure to the exterior violated all the canons of conservation and reconstruction, destroying completely the original harmony of the buildings on the Square.
>
> ..., in less than two decades, evidence of overcrowding again appeared (Lingelbach, "Philosophical Hall," 54).

Upon the completion of the addition, supporters of the Independence Hall preservation movement were highly offended not only by the "architecture" but also because the Society rented additional space to commercial interests. There was an effort to force the Society from the State House Square. This subsided and the American Philosophical Society had a few years of grace to seek a better solution to its housing needs.

The celebration of the Centennial of American Independence in Philadelphia during the summer of 1876 set off an anniversary frenzy that stimulated the nation's patriotic, historical, and promotional appetites. There were famous extravaganzas like the World's Columbian Exposition held at Chicago in 1893 and lesser known ones like that of August 1887 when "the Village of Lititz, in Lancaster County, Pennsylvania, celebrated its one-hundredth birthday" (Kammen, *Chords of*

Memory, 141). The American Philosophical Society went right along with the rest of the United States by celebrating the Centennials of its Incorporation (1880), the first meeting in Philosophical Hall (1889), Franklin's death (1890), and the Sesquicentennial of the Society's Founding (1893). One marvels at the vast quantities of Tortue Verte Claire, Selle de Venaison, Faisans Rotis, Terrapin à la Philadelphie, Pouding Glacé à la Philosophical, hock and champagne consumed by members (including some of the city's leading physicians) at the November 21, 1889 dinner at the Hotel Stratford and the equally splendid food and drink downed at the other anniversaries.

These meetings were extremely important for the Society's future development as they repeatedly emphasized its history and mission in a variety of ways while establishing precedent and experience for the great 1906 Bicentennial of Franklin's birth. The 1893 celebration of the Society's founding was far grander than anything attempted before. Held in Philosophical Hall over a five-day period, it was attended by members, representatives of fifty-six North American and European societies and institutions of higher education, and other guests. Eleven addresses, twelve formal papers, photographs, and reports, filled a 647-page commemorative volume of *Proceedings*. The philosophers and their guests attended eight receptions and open houses, including a visit to the technologically advanced Cramp's Ship Yard. While the focus of this celebration was scientific, the other anniversary gatherings were more varied with papers on the Society's history figuring prominently.

The founding of the American Historical Association in 1884 marked the rise of professionalism in the field of history. The American Philosophical Society began electing leading university trained historians like Herbert Baxter Adams (APS 1886) of Johns Hopkins. When the American Historical Association appointed its Historical Manuscript Commission to promote the collection, editing, and publication of American historical documents in 1895, the Society responded two years later by creating the Committee on Historical Manuscripts to

Fig. 8. Philosophical Hall with 1890 third story Library addition before renovation of 1949.

Fig. 9. Interior view of 1890 third story Library addition of Philosophical Hall.

Fig. 10. Meeting Room decorated for Sesquicentennial Celebration of 1893. View looking southwest. From American Philosophical Society, *Proceedings* 32 (1893).

examine the Library's historical documents and its early American imprints and consider ways to make them more available for study.

Thus the physical needs of the Library led to a deeper appreciation of the significance of its holdings; the anniversary meetings glorified the Society's past; and the development of professional American history caused the Society to consider ways its great book and manuscript collections, a critical source of the nation's history, might serve scholarship, the general public, and the organization itself in the future. Three men who would make the most of such promising situations were already at hand: two physicians and a biologist — Isaac Minis Hays (APS 1886), Francis X. Dercum (APS 1892) and Edwin G. Conklin (APS 1897). They were to effect a number of monumental changes at the American Philosophical Society during the first half of the twentieth century that was about to open.

Renewal and Redefinition, 1900-1942

More than fifty years now had passed since hands-on science was done in Philosophical Hall. The Society began the new century as a predominantly general scientific organization with a largely impressive honorary membership. It held meetings and published respectable if not distinguished journals in an historic headquarters already outgrowing the space provided by the 1890 stop-gap measure of the box-like third story. Shortly "a decided change" would occur "in the attitude of some of the officers and members of the Society towards the Hall" as they contemplated the increasingly unsatisfactory quarters. (Lingelbach, "Philosophical Hall," 54).

During the first forty years of the century the transformation of the Society was phenomenal. This was one of the most interesting and creative periods of the American Philosophical Society's history as well as the least well known. In retrospect, it can be seen that the Society had four major sets of needs and goals: to build at last a modern facility to satisfy its physical requirements for the foreseeable future; to develop new roles or functions and revitalize or discard traditional ones; to raise sufficient financial resources to achieve the first two goals; and to create a strong national and international reputation which would add credibility to fund-raising efforts. By 1940 all but the first challenge had been successfully met. That quest for adequate quarters would last nearly the entire century ending only with the successful completion of the Benjamin Franklin Hall project in time for the Society's 250th Anniversary Celebration in April 1993.

Much of the Society's success in the early twentieth century was due to the imaginative and energetic leadership of I. Minis Hays. Hays was a perfect match for the Society at that moment. A Philadelphian who received his medical education at the University of Pennsylvania, Hays later became the editor of the *American Journal of Medical Sciences.* Skills gained in this job served him well when he edited and published historical documents in the Society's library, prepared calendars of several large collections, and edited both the *Proceedings* and the *Transactions* (1898-1922). Hays received excellent organizational experience as Secretary-General of the International Medical Congress held in conjunction with the Philadelphia 1876 Centennial. As Librarian from 1897 to 1922, he brought order out of chaos, discovered the dimensions and richness of the collections, and undertook the first steps in needed conservation of rarities. I. Minis Hays was a shaper and executor of key Society policy. One might think of him as the Society's first modern administrator, a sort of proto-combination of today's Executive Officer and Librarian. The Committee on Historical Manuscripts was suggested by Hays in 1897 not only for sound scholarly reasons, but also with an eye to engaging the interest of the membership and the historical profession in the Society's collections and new publication efforts. In 1901, Hays formally proposed the idea of an annual meeting as a strategy to increase interest in the Society further by making it worthwhile and attractive for non-resident members to come to Philadelphia. Hays would also be instrumental in the planning, execution, and publication of the proceedings of the 1906 Bicentennial of Franklin's birth.

To give the Annual General Meeting and the Society the desired national flavor and scope, advantage was taken of a recent development in America's cultural life — the rise of great research universities. High quality faculties were being created throughout the United States, which presented the American Philosophical Society with a larger and more varied pool of candidates for election. Soon, the membership began to assume a more national character. The first Annual General Meeting of April 1902 was a great success. One hundred and fifteen members, many from outside the Philadelphia area, met for three days to hear papers and conduct the Society's business in a fashion strikingly similar to today's practice. The new national emphasis was reflected in the range of the speakers' institutions and those elected to membership. For example, election was made an annual event and the Laws were amended to limit election of residents of the United States to fifteen each year, and of foreign members to five. In 1918, the Laws restricted the total numbers of residents to 400 and foreign members to seventy-five. Over the years these rules have been changed to reflect the changing needs and circumstances of the Society. In 1906, the General Meeting was made consecutive with the National Academy of Sciences' spring Washington gathering (a practice that continues today); this increased the Philadelphia attendance of scientists from all parts of the nation.

The Annual General Meeting of 1906 celebrated Franklin's Bicentennial in a style unmatched until the 250th Anniversary Celebration. I. Minis Hays and other leaders of the Society apparently considered the meeting also in terms of future fund-raising to rebuild Philosophical Hall or construct a larger facility elsewhere. There was talk of designating the Society as the Franklin National Memorial; this definitely would have called for a new building, perhaps located on the recently proposed Benjamin Franklin Parkway. An application was made to the legislature of Pennsylvania to fund such a project in the amount of $350,000; in the end it appropriated one-tenth of the request, from which the governor released $20,000 to help mark Franklin's birth. The United States Congress, however, authorized a commemorative medal designed by Louis and Augustus St. Gaudens. One gold copy was presented, "under the direction of" President Theodore Roosevelt (APS 1904), to the Republic of France. One hundred fifty copies were struck in bronze, of which fifty were given to the American Philosophical Society for its use. Today the Franklin Medal is the Society's highest award in the sciences and the humanities. The scholarly events and the festivities in 1906 were impressive and some of the papers on aspects of Franklin's career and the state of human knowledge proved to be significant. Two universities bestowed honorary degrees, representatives of universities and sister learned societies throughout the world were in attendance, and a special concert was performed by the Philadelphia Orchestra. The proceedings were published in 1908 as *The Franklin Bicentennial Celebration* in conjunction with I. Minis Hays's superb four-volume *Calendar of the Franklin Papers*. If not exactly a household name, the Society's history and reputation had been enhanced greatly.

The decade before the outbreak of the First World War saw the Society engaged in a number of scientific and scholarly initiatives of national importance. Under the auspices of the Committee on Historical Manuscripts, the publishers Dodd, Mead & Company issued Reuben Gold Thwaites's eight-volume edition of the journals of the Lewis and Clark Expedition in 1904-1905, comprised mainly of the materials Jefferson had sent to the Society in 1817. Four years later the Society created the Committee on South Polar Exploration which attempted to foster a cooperative effort with other scientific and geographical societies to encourage the federal government to undertake an expedition to Wilkes Land and other areas of Antarctica.

The most dramatic and consequential event of these years occurred on November 24, 1911 when the American Philosophical Society entered into an agreement with the City of Philadelphia whereby the city would acquire Philosophical Hall and its lot, and in return would grant to the Society a site on the north side of Benjamin Franklin Parkway bordered by Sixteenth and Cherry Streets. On this triangular site it was "proposed to erect a dignified building, absolutely fire-proof, which shall be the home of the Society forever, and at the same time a permanent memorial to Benjamin Franklin, its founder, and thus commemorate for all time its founder, Benjamin Franklin, his lifelong services to science, to the State and Nation" (*Franklin*

House Plea, 39). In this somewhat florid manner, the Society in its first fund-raising appeal pamphlet, called on the public for support. Previously, the Special Committee on the Site for a New Hall had conducted a thorough study with the assistance of two leading Philadelphia architectural firms to learn whether Philosophical Hall could be rebuilt to provide for a good-size meeting room, a 200,000 volume book stack, a general reading room, a museum for the Society's cabinet and instruments, a council room, and administrative offices. While this was found to be technically possible, it could not be justified on financial or aesthetic grounds. The Committee recommended that no more money should be spent on Philosophical Hall and that a deal be struck with the City (*New Hall Site Committee*, 3-16). The Society's Council accepted these findings. This agreement with the city would remain in effect — determining the general path the Society would pursue for two decades — until 1936, when it was abrogated and the title to the Hall and the lot was confirmed by a city ordinance.

The Society's plan of 1911 to join the parade of Philadelphia cultural institutions to new homes on the Parkway stalled almost at once. "There the matter stood for fourteen years," until the Council in March 1925 reconfirmed the decision to move and Eli Kirk Price (APS 1916), the Society's treasurer, "was dispatched to discuss" the project with Paul P. Cret (APS 1928), one of America's leading architects (Brownlee, *City Beautiful*, 81).

The First World War would have a dramatic impact on the nature and future development of American society, economy, and culture, the nation's science and higher learning, and eventually on the American Philosophical Society itself. The war years saw the Society moving towards a higher level of public visibility. In May 1914, on the recommendation of a special committee, the Society adopted 1727, the date Franklin established the Junto, as its new founding date. The abandonment of 1743 was part of a national trend whereby many universities and colleges moved to establish (often speciously)

55

their greater antiquity. This decision allowed the Society to celebrate its Bicentennial in 1927 rather than sixteen years later, thus providing an appropriate occasion to launch a campaign to pay for the move to the Parkway if the requisite funds had not been secured by then. The conflict in Europe and America's entry into the war was to delay the entire Parkway project with the key structure, the Philadelphia Museum of Art, uncompleted until 1928.

The American Philosophical Society joined the National Research Council in 1916, which had been organized by the National Academy of Sciences to promote cooperation between governmental, educational, industrial, and other research organizations involved in scientific activities. Three years later the Society combined with eleven other scholarly organizations to found the American Council of Learned Societies, thus assuming a more prominent role in supporting the nation's humanities and social sciences. The three oldest founders — the Society, the American Academy of Arts and Sciences, and the American Antiquarian Society — were honorary bodies; the balance were professional societies.

Early in 1925, with the Society's Bicentennial only two years away, the Committee on Building and Site came to life again, primarily through the vigorous efforts and advocacy of Treasurer Eli Kirk Price and Vice President Francis X. Dercum. Price, a skillful lawyer and one of Philadelphia's most influential and effective civic leaders, was a man of intelligence, energy, and immense determination. His grandfather had helped found the Fairmount Park system and Price continued the family tradition of service as the dominant leader of both the Fairmount Park Commission and the entire Benjamin Franklin Parkway project. While Eli Kirk Price's major achievement was guiding the great Philadelphia Museum of Art to its completion at the head of the Parkway, he also campaigned tirelessly from 1911 onward to move "nearly a score of other institutions" — the American Philosophical Society among them — to "the new avenue and around Logan Circle" (Brownlee, *City Beautiful*, 45-70; 71 quote).

Francis X. Dercum received his medical degree from Pennsylvania in 1877 and then completed his doctorate in science. He worked with Joseph Leidy in comparative anatomy at the Academy of Natural Sciences, where he was elected a member in 1878. Dercum's research interests, which focused on the structure of the brain, led him into neurological science as a practitioner and a medical writer. He carried on an active practice and teaching career at Jefferson Medical College where in 1892 he was appointed Clinical Professor of Neurology and head of the Department of Nervous and Mental Diseases. Although only four years older than his collaborator, Dercum seemed to hail from a more courtly era than the hard-driving Price. Francis X. Dercum is recalled as a dignified, courteous, and kindly "professor" who was devoted to the Society's needs. During his presidency from April 1927 to his death four years later, Dercum arrived at Philosophical Hall by limousine at eleven o'clock sharp, said good morning to the staff working in the north room of the second floor, before proceeding to the Members' Room to the south where he spent exactly one hour conducting Society business. As his health became more fragile, Dercum was often accompanied by his personal nurse who awaited him in the staff office.

As previously noted, the Council in March 1925 had authorized Price to approach the great Beaux-Arts architect, Paul Cret, with an eye to having him produce a preliminary report and drawings for the Parkway site. Price, who had managed the situation brilliantly, now turned to a friend he had relied on heavily for advice and who designed several buildings for the Parkway. Over the years, the Society had assessed its physical needs for the future, which Price communicated to Cret as: "two auditoriums (seating one-hundred and three-hundred respectively), a library with a bookstack that could be expanded to hold a half million volumes, an exhibition gallery, a dining room, offices, conference rooms, and a residence to be used by the librarian or the secretary" (Brownlee, *City Beautiful*, 81). Later Cret was asked also to develop space for a broadcasting studio.

The Committee on Building and Site had "expressed themselves informally as in favor of a colonial style of architecture" — a style which Cret did not feel was particularly appropriate for the building although his first design aimed at satisfying the philosophers' taste. A contract was signed with Cret in May, and by December the Society had project drawings and a presentation perspective of a new Philosophical Hall that were expected to intrigue the membership.

The Bicentennial meeting of April 1927, if not as grand as the 1906 gatherings, was well attended by members, representatives of learned institutions from around the world, and other guests. Papers (a quarter now being in the social sciences and the humanities) were given in the hall and published as a special number of the *Proceedings;* dinners and other festivities were held elsewhere. Some "members..., crowded for space in the old Hall, were startled with the realization that a new building was an imperative need" (*Mankind Advancing*, 29). As had happened during previous major anniversary celebrations:

> the members took the occasion to review the Society's work and consider its future program. Many were apprehensive about the direction which science as a whole was taking and found they were dissatisfied with the Society's passive role in the movement. In particular, they sensed the growing apart of science and the humanities and felt that most laymen were insufficiently and improperly informed about the truths and meaning of scientific knowledge. The Philosophical Society, many felt, was uniquely qualified to address itself to these questions, to make, as one of them put it, "an inventory of the store of human knowledge," and outline the conquests of the future (Bell, "As Others Saw Us," 276).

Francis X. Dercum, the newly elected President, and Eli Kirk Price were prepared to capitalize on this heightened interest in the Society's responsibilities and future potential which they had helped to arouse. Cret's design for the new building was in hand — plans that the architect refashioned later in 1927 to conform more closely to his own neoclassical predilections. A campaign was called for to build and furnish the new Philosophical Hall and to endow its operation and future expansion of programs. But before mounting a drive which eventually would designate $1 million for construction and $1.25 million for endowment, Dercum and Price and their supporters believed that a "programme" of new, innovative activities needed to be articulated so as to capture the interest and open the checkbooks of major donors, some of whom might not be Society members. A Committee on Development led by Dercum spent the next two years formulating the "programme" and taking a fresh look at the Society's traditional activities.

First, the Committee on Development engaged in an "intellectual stock-taking" by asking the entire membership what "was the world's intellectual need," whether science and the humanities were drifting apart, whether specialization "in education and in thought" accelerated this process, and whether it might be possible to coordinate all knowledge into a single "programme with one common purpose — the promotion of useful knowledge?" By April 1929 about a quarter of the membership had responded; scientists generally were less concerned with the effects of specialization than were university presidents and humanists. Drawing on these observations and on its own investigations and discussions, the Committee set forth a "Three-Point Programme" that called for nothing less than the coordination of scientific and humanistic knowledge; the promotion of this coordinated knowledge through publications, meetings, and publicity (newspapers, magazines, radio, and movies); all of which was to take place in a "Clearing House of Knowledge" — a "Knowledge Bureau" — headquartered in the new Philosophical Hall on the Parkway. Exactly how this somewhat pretentious and rather naive scheme was to be carried out was explained only vaguely in the campaign literature and major publications. In a March 6, 1930 memorandum to Eli Kirk Price, the professional campaign director, Leslie S. Baker, confessed "that the Society's future programme of 'promoting useful knowledge' on a wider scale, has had little or no effect on larger donors." In short, the "programme" appears to have been a bust. Fortunately the case was also made that the Society's traditional functions would flourish in the new facilities and that for the first time there would be adequate space for a "larger public" to carry out research in the Society's collections and attend both scholarly and popular meetings. In the end, contributions were motivated by sentiment for the Society and what it had meant to Philadelphia for more than 200 years, by the obvious, pressing need for a new building, and by a desire to honor the memory of Benjamin Franklin.

The Society turned to the John Price Jones Corporation to develop and run a $2.25 million campaign between October 1929 and June 1930. Its archives picture a well organized, professionally conducted operation, (strikingly similar conceptually to the recently completed Benjamin Franklin Hall effort). The drive was announced formally a few days before the stock market crash ushered in the Great Depression. Despite a worsening economy, by November 1930, 337 contributors had pledged $1.12 million, of which half had been paid to the Society. Additionally, the Carnegie Corporation had given $100,000 for the use of the Library outside of the campaign proper. In time, the Society received the balance of the pledged funds. It was an extremely creditable achievement, which witnessed along the way some other extraordinary accomplishments and events.

The major campaign publications, *Mankind Advancing* and *When Aristotle Comes Again*, together with the campaign stationery were illustrated with Cret's 1929 presentation perspective of his neoclassical design. "Since January 1929, a regular news service ... resulted in the publication of the Society's activities in 1,346 listed newspapers. Newspaper clippings received show[ed] 5,409 news stories and 1,763 editorials all except three favorable to the Society and the campaign." The major donors may not have been excited by the "programme" but editors across the country certainly were. The Society joined with the National

Broadcasting Corporation in presenting four programs featuring distinguished members that were heard by "radio audiences of more than 34 broadcasting stations as far away as San Antonio, Texas." Isaiah Bowman's broadcast on Antarctica even reached the First Byrd Expedition at its base camp Little America (John Price Jones Corporation memorandum [May 16, 1930]). Dercum conceived of the broadcasts from Philosophical Hall as an example of what could be expected from the proposed "Knowledge Bureau." Perhaps more Americans in 1929-30 read or heard about the Society than at any other time in its history. Tradition was shattered on April 2, 1930 when the American Philosophical Society staged its first major meeting outside of Philadelphia; a gala reception and dinner was held at the Plaza Hotel in New York ostensibly to celebrate the 150th anniversary of its charter, but unabashedly to woo wealthy New Yorkers. For as Roland S. Morris (APS 1922) "cheerfully admitted," that was where "the money was" (Bell, "As Others Saw Us," 277). Seventy-one percent of the total contributions was the result of three gifts: Eldridge Reeves Johnson (APS 1925), the campaign treasurer, $500,000; Cyrus H.K. Curtis (APS 1930), $200,000; and Charles F. Brush (APS 1910), $100,000. Non-member gifts accounted for slightly less than a third of the grand total and non-Philadelphian gifts more than a quarter.

Cyrus Curtis, the eminent Philadelphia publisher, might have been even more generous to the Society if it had agreed to re-locate on the southwest corner of the block designed for the Franklin Institute's use. Curtis, who was interested in establishing a great national memorial to Benjamin Franklin in Philadelphia, offered to contribute $1 million to the cause if the American Philosophical Society, the Franklin Institute, and the Poor Richard Club, (a group of Philadelphia advertising and media men) joined forces with him. A tentative plan called for Paul Cret to oversee the entire project in which a statue of Franklin would be placed between the two buildings; the Poor Richard Club would help to raise the Society's share of the necessary funds (Cyrus Adler to Horace C. Richards, July 26,

1927). Negotiations between the Society and the Poor Richard Club were non-productive. In the end, this scheme of creating a constellation of institutions honoring the great man was realized partially in June 1928 when Cyrus Curtis gave $2 million to establish the Benjamin Franklin Memorial Corporation within the Franklin Institute buildings.

The deaths of Francis X. Dercum, Richard A.F. Penrose, and Eli Kirk Price in the early thirties altered the pace and direction of the American Philosophical Society's development. President Dercum died in Franklin's library chair while presiding over the opening of the Annual General Meeting on April 30, 1931. Having just expressed his belief that the Society would realize its ambitious expectations, Dercum's heart stopped. By the cruelest of ironies, when the morning session resumed, a life insurance executive delivered a paper entitled "Lengthening the Span of Life" which was broadcast by the National Broadcasting Company. One of the Society's most acute chroniclers has written that after the tragic event "the drawings of the great building were laid away ..., and Dr. Dercum's grand scheme for receiving, coordinating, evaluating and publishing new knowledge was quietly and completely forgotten (Bell, "As Others Saw Us," 277). But there was more to the story than that. The Parkway project was pursued actively until November 1933; as a result of the leadership of Dercum, Price, and their colleagues, the Society was prepared better "to define its proper role in the twentieth century" when Penrose died three months later on July 31, 1931, dividing his residuary estate of $7.8 million between the Geological Society of America and the American Philosophical Society for the creation of endowment funds.

Richard A.F. Penrose, a Philadelphian by birth, was a brother of the Republican political leader Boies Penrose. After receiving his A.B. and Ph.D. in geology at Harvard, he worked for the Texas, Arkansas, and United States geological surveys and also served as professor of economic geology at Chicago (1892-1911). In 1896 Penrose commenced his commercial geological activities in western mining properties which led him to found the Commonwealth Mining and Milling and Utah Copper companies. Thirty years later he had amassed a considerable fortune. His magnificent bequest to the Society was worth almost $4 million. The Society's leadership was pleasantly stunned and somewhat perplexed as how best to proceed. Penrose, who had become a member in 1905, was known to have been wealthy and interested in the Society. He was fully aware of the purposes and financial goals of the 1929-31 building and endowment campaign. His name appears on potential major donor lists, but Price's personal solicitation yielded only a very modest contribution of $300. It was — and is — not actually known why Penrose acted in such a generous manner although in 1945, Edwin G. Conklin speculated, "There is reason to believe that this campaign was a factor in leading" Penrose to write his will as he did ("Morris Biographical Memoir," 394). Perhaps it was the Society's new-found energy and discussion of future initiatives and service which motivated Penrose. The Society, however, now faced a dilemma. The campaign contributions and the Penrose bequest appeared to allow the Society to build and endow the Parkway project and still have in excess of $2.5 million left to support new activities such as research grants, while maintaining its traditional functions more generously than before. The sticking point was Penrose's earlier apparent lack of enthusiasm for the proposed new Philosophical Hall as demonstrated by his campaign gift. It was decided to study the overall situation carefully while allowing only $100,000 of Penrose funds to be spent on furnishing and equipping the new building and also creating some sort of a memorial there for the Society's great benefactor.

The growing dissatisfaction of non-Philadelphia members with the entire Parkway scheme and with the local leadership was an additional factor that held the Society back from assigning more Penrose funds. Hints of disenchantment, which surfaced during the campaign, now were transformed into blunt objections. Some members strongly recommended that if a nearby home for the Library could be acquired, such as the old

Second Bank of the United States, Philosophical Hall should be restored to its pre-1890 state and the Society remain in Old Philadelphia. This anti-Philadelphia sentiment may have spilled over into the December 4, 1931 presidential election to fill out Dercum's term, (which for some reason was delayed nine months). A local member with a reputation for imperious behavior was a candidate and likely to be elected if the usual low monthly stated meetings attendance prevailed. A counter-movement was formed, telegrams urged out of town members to attend, and eighty-seven members (twenty-three being non-Philadelphians) elected Princeton's Henry Norris Russell (APS 1913), America's leading theoretical astronomer, to serve until April 1932. Nearly all the Princeton members traveled to Philadelphia for the occasion. A minute in memory of Penrose was presented as was "a tentative list of members representing the different branches of learning to constitute a Committee on Policy to discuss the Society's future activities."

During this period, Paul Cret was responding to the Committee on Building and Site's July 1931 request to cut the Librarian's apartment from the architectural program while reviewing and rejecting the old concept of rebuilding Philosophical Hall to accommodate all the Society's activities. Satisfied, the Committee and the Council once again decided to proceed with the building on the Parkway. Cret was authorized in March 1932 to commence detailed working drawings. The building committee approved each set of interior drawings as they were completed. Momentum was mounting and "it appeared that the final resolution was nearing." In the fall, preliminary steps were taken to solicit construction bids from contractors (Brownlee, *City Beautiful*, 83). Meanwhile in May 1932, it was reported in the policy committee that construction costs might be reduced thirty percent due to the program's reduction and the deflationary impact of the Depression. A city ordinance authorized the exchange of the Philosophical Hall for the Parkway site, and on March 16, 1933 the Art Jury approved the design. Then the tide turned. A taxpayer's suit was instituted claiming that the land swap was fraudulent because the city was exchanging a prime "piece of property worth $900,000 for an old building whose value was $50,000 or less." The Society's lawyers felt certain that a favorable outcome could be achieved in time although they were concerned about obtaining clear title to a portion of the Parkway property. The philosophers were becoming upset by the publicity generated by the suit. Eli Kirk Price, the one man who might have driven the Parkway project to a successful conclusion, had died on January 24, 1933, which further dispirited the Society. These events, combined with the request of "members from outside Philadelphia who wished to retain the historic address," caused the Society effectively to abandon the great enterprise by the end of 1933. It was decided to ask the contributors "whether or not they would be content with remodeling the present Hall and building a fireproof Library" nearby (Building Committee Minutes, October 13, 1933). Later, Paul Cret would again serve as the Society's architect when renovating Philosophical Hall (Brownlee, *City Beautiful*, 83-85).

Meanwhile Edwin Grant Conklin (APS 1897) stepped forward in 1932 to become one of the most effective and influential leaders of the American Philosophical Society in the twentieth century. A major figure in American biology and a long-time faculty member at Princeton, Conklin played an increasingly dominant role in determining the Society's future direction for the next twenty years. Edwin Conklin's first introduction to the Society was in 1897 when, as a newly arrived young professor at Pennsylvania, he was invited by William Pepper (APS 1870) — the university's former distinguished Provost — to participate in the symposium on "Factors of Organic Evolution" with Cope and other notable scientists. Conklin was "flabbergasted" and tried to "beg-off." Pepper regretted Conklin's decision because "we had hoped to get acquainted with you"; Conklin took the hint, gave an impressive paper from the embryological point of view (later he called it "the only modern paper on the program"), and was promptly

Fig. 11. Edward Grant Conklin. Oil portrait on canvas by
Cameron Burnside, 1941 (American Philosophical Society).

elected to the Society. Woodrow Wilson (APS 1897) President of
Princeton, in 1908 invited Conklin to Princeton where he built

up the biology department's strengths while serving as chairman for twenty-five years (Bonner and Bell, "What is Money For," 79-80). From the time of his election onward, Conklin played an active role in the Society's affairs as a member of important standing committees and as an officer from 1901 until six months prior to his death in November 1952. He was Vice President from 1932 to 1942, served as the first Executive Officer from 1936 to 1942, and was President in 1942-1945 and 1948-1952 (the only person in the Society's history to serve two non-sequential terms). Suddenly presented in 1950 with the opportunity to acquire a major collection of Darwin correspondence, Conklin, on the recommendation of Librarian William E. Lingelbach, did so immediately, thereby laying the foundation of the Library's great holdings in evolutionary thought, of which he was one of his generation's outstanding interpreters.

Conklin had a deep interest in the philosophical and historical aspects of science and a life-long devotion to the classics. When speaking as outgoing President of the American Association for the Advancement of Science, Conklin said, "There is no excuse for the scientist who dwells permanently apart from the affairs of men" ("Conklin Biographical Memoir," 10-11). He was clearly an excellent person to help direct the fortunes of the American Philosophical Society in the 1930s and 1940s as it made the transition to a multi-disciplinary learned society dedicated, in the words of its Charter, to "the prosecution and advancement of all useful branches of knowledge."

From 1932 to 1942 Conklin worked productively in tandem with President Roland S. Morris. The two men got on famously and together they guided the American Philosophical Society through one of the most significant periods of its long history. Conklin concentrated on the restructuring of the scholarly organization while Morris devoted himself to the financial and legal challenges resulting from the Society's growing endowment and broadened activities. When Morris retired from the presidency (to be succeeded by Conklin) the Society's investments had grown to nearly $7 million. Conklin's 1945 biographical memoir of Morris, distinguished by the author's admiration of and affection for his friend, concisely reviews those years' achievements while generously ascribing most of the credit to his co-worker.

Roland Morris was a man of great national and local stature, a fact that helped assure the non-Philadelphians that the interests of the entire membership would be well served. Following graduation from the University of Pennsylvania Law School in 1899, he helped found Duane, Morris & Heckscher, which became one of Philadelphia's leading law firms. As an undergraduate at Princeton, Morris was deeply impressed by the teaching of Woodrow Wilson, especially his doctrine that Princetonians' duty as citizens was to take an active role in politics and government. Starting at the ward level, Morris became a leader of the reform wing of the state Democratic party, serving as the State Chairman and a delegate to four National Democratic Conventions. During the election of 1912 he became a close associate of Woodrow Wilson, who named Morris as Ambassador to Japan in 1917. In this role Morris made three lengthy secret missions to Siberia for the President to investigate the "White" Russian counter-revolutionary movement. Upon his return to private life, in 1921, Morris devoted himself to his growing law practice and a broad range of local, national, and international activities of a professional, civic, and religious nature.

Roland Morris's contributions to the American Philosophical Society, to which he was elected in 1922, were numerous. Most notable was his ordering of the Society's finances and endowment. Through his good offices the Society received a bequest from Judson Daland, a Philadelphia physician, in 1937 establishing a fund for the promotion of research in clinical medicine. That year Morris also successfully engineered the transfer of the building campaign's subscriptions to the endowment, with the understanding that these gifts "might be used for the future erection of a building which would be a monument to Franklin, and which would provide for the

Library, and for other activities of the Society" (Shryock, "Planning Library Hall," 350).

The Committee on Policy went to work in April 1932 after canvassing its membership for ideas about the Society's future. This committee (1932-33), together with standing committees, special committees and subcommittees, investigated and debated all aspects of the Society's mission and operations and recommended policies to the leadership and the broader membership. Adopted in the ensuing years to 1941, they laid the foundation of the modern Society. The Committee on Policy was transformed quickly into a seven-person executive committee with the President and the Secretaries serving ex officio. The Executive Committee met regularly with the building and finance committees as long as the Parkway project was alive to guarantee the Society's scholarly and social requirements were coordinated with the architectural program. During the initial meetings, members raised issues and specific proposals that later would be considered in greater detail before being accepted, amended, or rejected. It quickly became evident that the Society did not possess a committee system which represented the interests of all the members. The Subcommittee on the Division of Members into groups called for the appointment of an Advisory Committee on the Promotion of Knowledge organized in four sections which corresponded to the membership Classes established in 1936. Thus even before the Laws were changed that classification system was employed to facilitate thinking about publications, meetings, the Library and the possibility of a research grants program, coordinating scientific abstracting services, and establishing yearly symposia on critical scientific and humanistic topics.

The policy, finance, and building committees quickly turned their attention to *the* critical issue — the resolution of which determined how the Society might proceed with its programmatic development — the use of the Penrose bequest income on which there were no testamentary restrictions. It was "decided that the primary obligation of the Society was, in the language of Franklin, 'the promotion of useful knowledge,' and that the income...must be devoted in large part to 'the increase of knowledge through investigation'; and that not more than $100,000 of the income be used for the new building and its equipment ("Morris Biographical Memoir," 395). In due course, "the increase of knowledge through investigation" was translated into the support of research, the selective publication of such research, and meetings, where the results of research were reported and discussed. While all manner of good things flowed from this major decision, reaching those final goals was no easy task. The debate was frank, often very sharp, and Conklin and Morris needed all their wit, patience, and diplomatic skills to sort out the ideas and opinions of a newly energized membership. The players in this game were skilled and knowledgeable, being some of the nation's leading scientists, scholars, university presidents and deans, research institution directors, and top foundation administrators. The upper echelon of the American academic world was still relatively small and compact in the 1930s; for the balance of the decade the American Philosophical Society could draw on the services of many of this rather small group. The Second World War radically changed that environment and the Society, while ably served by it members, could never again make such extraordinary claims on the time of men and women in mid-career.

How the Society revamped and modernized both its membership and meetings can be told as a single tale. Now that the Society was more affluent, it was proposed to the Committee on Policy in May 1932 that initiation fees and annual dues be abolished. President Morris did not think that the moment was propitious, pointing out that the finance committee "was against [it] ... not on account of the small financial return but because they thought it bad psychology." This fiscal restraint was abandoned four years later, when these charges were dropped at the same time that other long-time sources of income, the leases of Philosophical Hall were given up. In 1934, the American Philosophical Society terminated all leases with its tenants, thus assuming complete control of its headquarters for the first time since it was occupied 145 years earlier.

The Laws as amended April 24, 1936, stated that "every member, whether resident or foreign, shall be classified ... into the following four classes:"

Class I.   Mathematical and Physical Sciences
Class II. Geological and Biological Sciences
Class III. Social Sciences
Class IV. Humanities

The Class subdivisions were also set forth, as were the election procedures, steps for formal admission, the right of the Society to assess dues, and procedures for terminating the membership of a member, "for good and sufficient cause...." During the discussion of dividing the membership into groups, strong demands were made that the Society be restructured so as to strengthen the representation of the social sciences and the humanities. The leadership vowed to work to create a better balance and by 1941 progress clearly had been made. The Autumn General Meeting was inaugurated in November 1936; the stated monthly meetings were ended. The following year a two-day Midwinter meeting was held in February, a practice that continued until 1945. These popular gatherings were devoted to symposia, half of which were joint meetings with other organizations. These symposia, which resulted in notable Society publications, investigated such topics as "Publication of Research" (1938), (of great importance, they discussed microfilming and this led to formation of University Microfilms), "Life and Work of Elihu Thomson" and "Progress of Astrophysics" (1939), "One-Hundredth Anniversary of The Wilkes Naval Exploring Expedition, 1838-1842" (1940), "The Early History of Science and Learning in America, especially the work of the Society in the Eighteenth and Nineteenth Centuries" (1942), and "Postwar Problems" (1943).

When dues were ended, "the Society decided to provide hotel accommodations for its out-of-town members and invited

71

guests at the time of these meetings (a practice honored today). Thus the attendances and the programs were greatly improved ("Morris Biographical Memoir," 397). Edwin G. Conklin observed wryly in his April 1945 President's Report that these two actions made "membership in this Society more entirely honorary than any other learned society in this country." There had even been some thought of subsidizing the rail fare of members attending from a distance. As Conklin also pointed out, "until recently the cost of entertainment of out-of-town members and guests fell largely upon the local members, who subscribed generously for luncheons and dinners which in those earlier days far outshone in luxury our recent entertainments, while some of the local members gave memorable breakfasts and entertained in their homes distinguished members from a distance."

But all was not perfect in paradise. By the end of the decade, there was criticism that the quality of the meetings was uneven. Excellent papers often were followed by boring, amateur efforts. It was felt that the Committee on Meetings depended on members who volunteered their services and did not invite enough distinguished non-members to participate. A cursory comparison of programs with the resident membership list indicated a generous participation by members, as might be expected. On the other hand, the Committee on Meetings made a point of including numerous grant recipients so the Society could learn the results of their research (seventeen of twenty-six papers at the 1936 Autumn General Meeting). The leadership raised the perennial complaint that the Society should take care not to fill up its ranks with those taking no interest in its activities. Some twenty eight percent of those accepting election had failed to sign the roll and had not been admitted to full membership, seventy percent of this group had been elected for more than five years, "and most of them had never attended a meeting of the Society." The absence of initiation fees or annual dues, which previously discouraged the uninterested (but also tended to keep the Society a more local institution), allowed the

Society to carry such persons "as nominal members ... and thereby prevented the election of more active" ones (1945 *Year Book*, 35). One proposal (it has been put forward on several occasions since) was to exclude individuals from membership if they failed to sign the roll within five or ten years after election. Fortunately nothing has come of this suggestion because in this age of academic mobility and cheap airfares, there are numerous examples of men and women who became active in the Society after these suggested limitations would have taken effect and cut them from the rolls.

The American Philosophical Society took a pioneering step in 1933 by making a $3,000 grant to Thomas C. Poulter, physicist of the Second Byrd Antarctic Expedition, to acquire echo-sounding equipment for measuring the depth of the polar ice cap and discovering the nature of its basic support. This first research grant by the Society was rewarded with a short wave radio report from Poulter read at a January meeting, a full published account later, and forty-two reports on all aspects of the expedition published as the 1945 *Proceedings* No. 1, "Scientific Results of the U.S. Antarctic Service Expedition, 1934-4." Far more important, it inaugurated the program for which the Society is highly regarded throughout the academic world, and which during the succeeding sixty years distributed more than $15 million of awards to over 12,000 scientists and scholars. The Committee on Policy recommended in January 1933 that $20,000 a year of the Penrose Fund income be set aside to be administrated by the Committee on the Use of Funds for the Advancement of Knowledge Through Investigation; a year later this body was given the shorter name of the Committee on Grants. Initially there was a good deal of opposition to the establishment of a grants-in-aid program which, of course, was exactly what the Society's general grant program rapidly became. Some felt there were already sufficient opportunities of this nature available, that if the scholarly community became aware of the Society's intention to make modest grants-in-aid, it would be swamped with applications without a mechanism to handle the deluge.

Others proposed that a wiser course would be to limit awards to members themselves, or to the support of research of specific interest to the Society, or to substantial assistance to non-Society institutional investigation, or to the purchase of expensive equipment. The early grants, in fact, included examples of all these suggestions, but by the end of the practice was to make small grants of around $1,000 to individual scientists and scholars to assist them in carrying out their own research projects. By 1942 — after nine years of making grants — the American Philosophical Society had expended $712,600 of its income on research. Of this sum the Penrose Fund provided nearly $600,000 for 683 grants in more than forty different fields. Sixty-one grants totaling $77,020 were made from the Eldridge Reeves Johnson Fund, and the Judson Daland Fund made nine grants totaling $35,850 ("Morris Biographical Memoir," 396).

To further its understanding on how best to support research, the Society had earlier in 1937 sponsored a joint meeting with some thirty-five other organizations administering such programs. It was a landmark gathering, as one hundred and twenty-five persons spent two days participating in discussions and hearing papers in Philosophical Hall; those from out-of-town were guests of the Society. The nation's leading policymakers and administrators in the field (most of whom were or would become members), such as President Frederick P. Keppel (APS 1938) of the Carnegie Corporation and Warren Weaver (APS 1944) of the Rockefeller Foundation attended, together with the presidents of Michigan and the Massachusetts Institute of Technology, and the heads of the Smithsonian Institution, the National Academy of Sciences, the National Research Council, and the American Council of Learned Societies. Such a showing was a tribute to the new commitment of the American Philosophical Society. While no formal policy statements were issued, the entire landscape of the promotion of knowledge through research assistance was surveyed in "Round Table" discussions, formal addresses, and concentrated reviews of general topics. The Society was convinced that its grants-in-aid

74

could play a positive role between the level of great foundations and universities and that of research councils and other organizations. There was a general consensus that this type of support "could be made to benefit a much larger number of investigators than could fellowships, and that the needs and volume of such grants was very great." At the end of the day, the American Philosophical Society was reassured that it had created a well conceived and properly executed program thus taking "an important place among institutions ... administering funds in aid of research" (*Proceedings*, 77 [1937], 628-29). All things considered, the Society's record would be a remarkable and enviable achievement of which it could be justly proud.

The Penrose bequest also allowed the American Philosophical Society to adopt a creative and aggressive publication program. Discussions began at once in the Policy Committee and a subcommittee on publications was appointed to formulate an initial strategy for the Society's consideration. By 1937 publications had been restructured, redefined, and expanded, acquiring the general configuration of today's program. Then as now this was considered one of the most important activities of the Society (probably *the most important*), being "the chief means by which its purpose of promoting useful knowledge is extended through space and time. "Yet," as President Conklin observed in 1945, "There [was] no activity of the Society upon which so much difference of opinion exist[ed] among members" (1945 *Year Book*, 38). Only the Parkway project itself caused more vigorous debate and dissent in the 1930s.

The early discussions in the Policy Committee (were intriguing and) revealed not only what members judged valuable or significant in the publications, but also the extent of their ambitions. William B. Scott, (APS 1886), Chairman of the Policy Committee and Princeton geologist and paleontologist, claimed in May 1932 that "there was no other scientific organization that provided really good illustrations, especially of colored maps, and that he thought that if the Society would specialize on especially fine illustrations, it would be doing a very useful thing for the scientific world." He also suggested the *Proceedings* be published in disciplinary series. It was decided that a paid secretary to the publications committee would be more useful than a paid editor. The subcommittee made two general recommendations; the first, which was accepted, called for the publication of the *Proceedings* and *Transactions* "in the best possible style, and of such unusually meritorious monographs as may be appropriate to its field;" the second, which was laid on the table, urged providing a home in the Parkway building for the Chemical, Biological, Psychological Abstracts editorial offices and similar systems with an eye to effecting a grand unified and coordinated system. This plan certainly echoed something of Dercum's "Knowledge Bureau." The Advisory Committee on Promotion of Knowledge for its part recommended that a portion of Penrose Fund income be set aside to support publications of outstanding merit "in the most appropriate and adequate manner." By 1933 the stage was set for reforms which were completed by 1937. The *Transactions*, the nation's oldest learned journal which up to that time had been published sporadically in the twentieth century, was revived and regularized. Volumes or parts of volumes were to be monographs of at least one hundred pages. The *Proceedings* was revamped to contain ten to twenty-page papers presented at meetings, symposiums, external research communications, enlarged coverage of Society business, and obituaries of deceased members (biographical memoirs). Another series, the *Memoirs*, publishing scholarly books in all fields of learning, was inaugurated in 1935 with a mathematical treatise to which the present Executive Officer Herman H. Goldstine (APS 1979) gave "valuable editorial and mathematical assistance," thus commencing his long association with the Society. As the business of the Society accelerated and became more complex, in 1937 the *Year Book* also was established to contain an annual record of the Society's activities, including detailed reports of meetings, standing committees, finances, and also biographical memoirs, which were moved from the *Proceedings*. A major portion of each volume was dedicated to reports of grant recipients which informed the scholarly world what investigations were being supported by the Society. An editor, assisted by four Class editors, was appointed to oversee the general publication process. The 1936 amended Laws not only spelled out the responsibilities of the Committee on Publications, but also defined the nature of the publications themselves. There was a major expansion of published scholarly contributions during the first seven years of the 1930s (264 *Proceedings* papers, nine *Transactions,* and eight *Memoirs* by 160 members and 121 non-members). While the class memberships were not equal (Class I: thirty one percent, Class II: thirty eight percent, Class III: seventeen percent, and Class IV: fourteen percent) in 1937 Class III and Class IV combined equaled the other classes. The Society's journals published more than twice as many papers in Class II as in Class I or as in Class III and IV combined. Class II papers presented at meetings tended to be published while Class I papers were not. The overabundance of Class II papers and other perplexing issues caused many members to question whether the appropriate scholarship was being published by the American Philosophical Society and, if so, whether it was reaching its proper audience. Of course, this imbalance was not the result of any policy; the Society could publish only what it was given.

In 1935 it was proposed that all the Society's publications be divided into two series, A and B, the contributions in the fields of the first two Classes to be placed in the former category, and the last two Classes in the latter one. This was really an outgrowth of an earlier sentiment that the *Proceedings* be published in four Class series. The whole publication debate began in earnest at the 1937 Annual General Meeting at which time a special committee representing each Class and its subsections was appointed to consider the matter. When no agreement could be reached by this body, or by the Committee on Publications, or by an additional special committee, the general positions of all groups were presented at the 1938 February Midwinter meeting devoted to the publication of research with a special emphasis on the use of microfilm. The discussion of the Society's publications by members from all four Classes was extremely lively, frank, and at times even biting. It was discovered that distribution of the Society's publications was effected almost completely by domestic and foreign exchanges, with subscriptions playing a minor role (1940 exchanges to subscriptions ratios: *Proceedings* 662:60; *Transactions* 196:26). As the 1945 subcommittee on publications later observed about exchanges, "Many...went to institutions and organizations which are not ... active research centers, such as learned societies" (1945 *Year Book*, 108). Conklin made a determined effort to reverse this situation; which proved successful; by 1945, subscriptions had increased dramatically and exchanges were dropped if they lay outside the Library's collecting interests. Another method of distribution was at work, however. The Society's extremely generous reprint policy (*Transactions* fifty copies gratis; *Proceedings*, one hundred copies gratis; *Memoirs*, fifty copies gratis), allowed authors to place their work in colleagues' hands and in appropriate libraries. Furthermore members received a copy of every publication. But in 1938 there was still an uneasy feeling that some of the Society's publications were not reaching their intended audiences. A number of Class I members even went so far as to suggest caustically that some publications, though they reached their targets, aroused little interest.

The debate over the nature and quality of research that should be published was shaped in part by the Society's philosophical commitment to encompassing and supporting all fields of knowledge. Could a general learned society effectively publish advanced scholarship in many rapidly evolving, highly technical fields? Class I's subcommittee thought not, unless radical changes took place. It concluded "that the best interests of Class I ... [could] be served by the prompt publications of original scientific literature up to 25 pages in length, in several sciences comprised in Class I." Such literature would be contained in a monthly journal of 500 pages a year, and directed by a paid editor. The papers generally should embody the results of original research submitted by members. But this proposal did not receive unanimous approval by Class I. Some felt that Society funds would be better spent supporting the publication of research "in already established specialized scientific journals." Others supported the rapid publication of symposia on critical scientific problems or issues, a technique utilized successfully by the Faraday Society of London. It was, however, the "very definite view" of many members in the physical sciences that the *Proceedings*, "whatever the merit in the opinion of members of other sections of the Society, failed to reach those high standards of worth and scientific excellence ... to which it must be our constant effort as members of the Society to attain" (1938 *Year Book*, 90). Having called for a separate journal the Class I representatives were quick to concede that other publication options available to them were more than adequate (a happy circumstance also enjoyed by Class II members). For Class I it was a question of mounting a more than creditable effort or attending to other matters. The Class II subcommittee called for a variety of reforms, but stopped short of demanding its own journal. Classes III and IV were more or less satisfied with the status quo, although their representatives also advanced proposals for improving the Society's publications while fostering their disciplines' interests. These recommendations, discussions, and observations reveal the American Philosophical Society, searching for new goals while clinging to a familiar, tested path (1938 *Year Book*, 82-115).

Conklin stated the discussion's results showed that undertaking "the publication of specialized journals in the major fields represented by membership in the Society" would be unwise. To do so would certainly alter, and perhaps violate, the all-inclusive character of the Society which many members felt was one of its most attractive charms. For Conklin the job at hand was not only to improve the general quality of published papers within traditional formats, but to enlarge and reorient distribution. During the next seven years, he would achieve impressive results in the latter area.

Following the First World War, the Library increasingly came into its own. The Society's fund-raising efforts were predicated in part on providing safe, modern quarters for its books and manuscripts and their users. To that end, attention was repeatedly drawn to the Society's rarities: the Franklin Papers, the draft of the Declaration of Independence in Jefferson's hand, the Lewis and Clark journals, and the unique runs of journals of foreign scientific societies and learned academies. By the time of the United States' entry into the Second World War in 1941, the Society had formulated policies governing collection development, future facilities, and scholarly and public access. Thus the Library was poised to assume its place alongside the Society's major components—membership and meetings, publications, and research grants.

Four years after the retirement of Librarian I. Minis Hays in 1922, the Society, seeking to make the position more professional, amended the Laws so that Society membership was no longer a prerequisite. Laura E. Hanson was appointed and ably directed the Library and its small staff until 1942. Acid neutral paper folders were first employed in 1930 when the Archives and the Miscellaneous Manuscript Collections were catalogued. During the Thirties, the Library became one of the first American institutions to microfilm its collections for record, preservation, security purposes, and to make them available to scholars. Earlier in 1910 the third floor of Philosophical Hall had become jammed beyond its capacity, and books and pamphlets overflowed into the basement. Ten thousand of the rarest imprints were transferred to a bank vault, which precluded their use; this process was repeated several times during the next twenty years. The least used volumes were consigned to dead storage in a warehouse. "When the Society decided to remain in Philosophical Hall, the problem of housing the Library became acute." The Library moved in 1934 from Fifth Street to rented quarters across the street — the old Stock Exchange rooms of the Drexel Building — and resided there for over two decades. This solution, while not satisfactory in the long run, did provide ampler space which also was cleaner and more agreeable. "It also set a precedent — one can now see — for locating the Library elsewhere than in Philosophical Hall" (Shryock, "Planning Library Hall," 350).

The Drexel Building facilities allowed the Society to acquire important additions to the Library collections. In 1936 the Society purchased from a descendant about 1,100 Franklin manuscripts, thus augmenting the large Franklin collection (some 11,000 items) that was presented in 1840 by Charles Pemberton Fox and his sister Mary Fox of Philadelphia. The heirs of Elihu Thomson (APS 1876), the distinguished physicist, electrical inventor, and manufacturer, gave his great collection (55,000 items) to the Society in 1937. Eight years later the American Council of Learned Societies presented the papers of the famous anthropologist Franz Boas (APS 1903); they have become one of the Library's most consulted collections.

After 1934, the Committee on Library continually studied, analyzed, and discussed the needs and challenges of the Library. The Library program of Paul Cret's Parkway design that called for a 500,000 volume stack capacity, reading rooms, and exhibition facilities, as well as offices and technical spaces devoted to cataloguing, photography, and conservation, figured largely in the Committee's planning. By the end of the decade, the Society had reached the decision that the Library should be housed in its own building, separate from whatever form Philosophical Hall might take in the future (Shryock, "Planning Library Hall," 350). A special committee on collections' development spent a number of years analyzing the Library's holdings. Its report, which the Society adopted in 1941, called for the Library to develop into a research institution specializing in several areas, which they identified as Frankliniana; American Colonial and Revolutionary history; and Native American languages, archaeology, and ethnology.

With Pearl Harbor the United States went to war and the American Philosophical Society joined in with grim determination. Members and members-to-be — both men and women — served with distinction in all branches of the military and did invaluable work in the civilian war effort. Scientists contributed to top secret enterprises and economists, historians, art historians, archaeologists, and scholars with language skills gravitated to intelligence organizations such as the Office of Strategic Services, where they could bring their analytical skills and knowledge of foreign lands and cultures to bear. While most worked in offices in Washington or Allied nations, not a few men and women operated secretly in enemy and occupied territory. Recently some like Brooke Hindle (APS 1982), Paul Mellon (APS 1971), and Emanuel R. Piore (APS 1967) have written compellingly about their wartime experiences. A significant portion of the scientific story resides in the Society's manuscript collections. There within the papers of Henry DeWolf Smyth (APS 1947), Stanislaw M. Ulam (APS 1967), numerous others, and the Archives for the History of Quantum Physics is to be found valuable historical information about that great engine of war — the Manhattan Project — and other military related scientific and technological projects.

The conflict caused the Society to defer its plans to renovate Philosophical Hall and erect a separate Library building. Fearing that the Germans would attempt to bomb or destroy by sabotage America's national shrine, Independence Hall, the papers of Benjamin Franklin were removed from the Library's vaults in the Drexel Building during the war and stored for greater safety with the Fidelity-Philadelphia Trust Company. The business of the Society went on and even in the darkest days its focus was firmly fixed on the postwar challenges and problems of science, scholarship, and economic and political reconstruction.

The Modern Society, 1942-1993

During the next fifty years, the American Philosophical Society adhered with amazing fidelity to the course charted by the leadership of the 1930s. Edwin G. Conklin, Eli Kirk Price, and even Francis X. Dercum would be very much at home in today's Society — gratified, but not particularly surprised, by the accomplishments of the last half century. The membership itself grew and became more diverse. Women who first became resident members in 1869 were elected more frequently, and with the election of Ralph J. Bunche (APS 1950) an African American belatedly joined the Society's ranks. Even today the paucity of women and minority members is a matter of serious concern as the Society celebrates its 250th anniversary. The General Meetings were distinguished by important symposia on postwar problems, notable papers illuminating the Bicentennials of the Declaration of Independence and the Constitution, the inauguration of a home- and-home series of joint meetings with the Royal Society in 1980, and the great four-day gala of April 1993. The general grants and publications programs progressed along their respective paths in a steady and highly useful fashion. By 1945 a more equitable balance was achieved among the sciences and the social sciences and the humanities in the allocation of funds and coverage of these activities; by the early 1990s, sixty percent of general grants funds were supporting social science and humanities research and seventy five percent of publication space was devoted to these two areas of scholarly inquiry. With the introduction of the computer, the Committee on Research was able to evaluate the expanding number of grant applications more efficiently and quickly. By 1993 the Society's average general grant was worth less in constant dollars than in 1940 and the competition was much stiffer. However, the actual number of annual awards had increased nearly three-fold during the past half century. Special grants programs were established such as the Phillips Fund in Native American languages and ethnohistory, the John C. Slater Research Fund for doctoral fellowships in the history of modern physical science, and the Mellon Foundation Resident Research Fellowships for work in the Library's collections. The Publications Office paid more attention to the design, and the 1980s saw awards not only for scholarly quality of publications but also for attractive layout, illustrations, and typography. The requirement that authors submit their manuscripts on computer disks helped control editorial and composition costs. The Society also became an active partner in such scholarly enterprises as *The Papers of Benjamin Franklin, The Collected Letters of Charles Darwin, The Joseph Henry Papers, The Papers of Benjamin Henry Latrobe, The Journals of the Lewis and Clark Expedition*, and *The Collected Papers of Charles Willson Peale and his Family*.

The big story of these years, however, was the remarkable growth and renovation of the American Philosophical Society's physical facilities, and the necessary, accompanying development of financial resources that made possible new construction in the 1980s and early 1990s. This was surely the era of building the Society's history. In 1948-49, $215,476 was spent on removing the third floor from Philosophical Hall in order to restore the exterior to its pre-1890 state and thoroughly renovate the interior (later modern office space was created in the basement in 1986 and a new heating and air conditioning system installed in 1992). Library Hall, constructed for $2 million on the site of the old Library Company of Philadelphia building (1789-1884) in the Independence National Historical Park was opened November 11, 1959. The conservation lab was modernized and enlarged in 1986. The Society's third building, Benjamin Franklin Hall at 427 Chestnut Street (the former Farmers' and

Mechanics' Bank) was acquired in 1981 for Library and general Society use and reconstructed and restored in two phases: 1982-84 and 1990-93. Since 1977 a succession of Presidents, Executive Officers, Librarians and other Society leaders used their considerable planning and fundraising skills to bring the Chestnut Street projects to successful conclusions.

Another significant achievement of these years was the evolution of the Library into a national research center for the study of the history of science and early American history and culture. This was facilitated by a combination of factors: the policy initiated in 1942 of appointing respected historian-librarians who developed research collections and scholarly programs; the generous allocation of Society funds; and valuable external support from the Friends of the Library ($433,555 since 1970) and foundations — most prominently the Andrew W. Mellon Foundation's six grants that provided $900,000 for endowments and $1.1 million for programs. To provide the logistic support to maintain this programmatic momentum, the Society's small staff grew gradually and became highly professional. Today computer technology is a fact of life in every aspect of the Society's operations.

The American Philosophical Society has always been a supportive neighbor of Philadelphia's cultural and educational institutions. Since 1980, the Society has created a more formal outreach program. It has collaborated with other organizations in mounting major national exhibitions and staged its own shows; worked closely with the Philadelphia public school system in enhancing teachers' intellectual enrichment, and co-sponsored public affairs symposia and speeches in Philosophical Hall that are broadcast on local public radio. The usefulness and success of these undertakings among a wider audience than its own membership should figure significantly in future Society planning.

No leader was to dominate the Society following the second retirement of Conklin from the presidency in April 1952. Perhaps this was because the major programs' policies and goals — except those of the Library — were fairly well settled by the early 1950s, the distribution of responsibilities between Presidents and Executive Officers was achieved and a number of influential, and long-term committee chairmen emerged.

In these circumstances how best can the Society's leadership of the period be described? Sketches of three men — William E. Lingelbach (APS 1916; Librarian 1942-1958), Henry Allen Moe (APS 1943; President 1959-1970), and George W. Corner (APS 1940; Executive Officer 1960-1977) — that appear in the following narrative hopefully will capture some of the flavor of the times.

1942 - 1976

From April 24 to July 31, 1942, the American Philosophical Society in conjunction with the Worldwide Broadcasting Foundation produced a series of weekly short-wave broadcasts from Philosophical Hall "on Independence Square to those countries overseas" where the English language was spoken and understood and "where there [was] still an interest in the progress of science and learning and faith in that form of government which was established in this very place" (letterhead, broadcast news release, April 24, 1942). The message in Conklin's introductory broadcast and the fifteen subsequent addresses of series was clear: while science was an international enterprise it only could function properly in a world free of fascist totalitarianism. A second set of eight broadcasts a year later was factually straightforward without any ideological overtones. Shortly thereafter when the Office of War Information preempted all overseas short-wave broadcasts, "Radio Free APS" ceased operations.

Two timely symposia took place in 1943: the first in February on "Post-War Problems" — the other in November on the "Organization, Direction, and Support of Research"; and their papers were published in the 1944 *Proceedings*. But it was the Society's April 1943 Bicentennial of Thomas Jefferson's birth that is most germane in 1993. It produced a set of papers,

Fig. 12. April 1942 Annual General Meeting. Group outside of west facade of Philosophical Hall. Seated center from left: W.F.G. Swan, Secretary; Roland S. Morris, President; Edwin G. Conklin, President-elect and Executive Officer; Luther P. Eisenhart, Executive Officer-elect.

illuminating the great Virginian's amazing, multifaceted career — perhaps the best known today being that of the Cornell historian Carl Becker (APS 1936) "What is Still Living in the Political Philosophy of Thomas Jefferson?" As the Society already had celebrated a Bicentennial in 1927 sixteen years earlier, the focus of the meeting was on Jefferson's numerous accomplishments — among them his role in shaping the Society as its third President. Conklin clearly indicated his view of the 1727 founding date when in his introduction he stated "the real bicentennial of the Society" — 1743 — would "be celebrated at the dinner at the close of the third day." Others must have shared Conklin's sentiment, for in 1948 the Society voted to confirm 1743 as its founding date.

In August 1945 the Second World War was ended by the American atomic bomb attacks on Hiroshima and Nagasaki. Three months later a symposium on "Atomic Energy and its Implications," sponsored jointly by the Society and the National Academy of Sciences, was held in Philosophical Hall on November 16 and 17. This was one of the first public conferences devoted to the atomic bomb, and it featured papers by such key figures as J. Robert Oppenheimer (APS 1945), Enrico Fermi (APS 1939), Eugene P. Wigner (APS 1944), Harold C. Urey (APS 1935), John Archibald Wheeler (APS 1951), Arthur H. Compton (APS 1925), and Henry D. Smyth. To read the symposium's papers today is like attending the end of the first act of a terrifying, tortuous but fascinating play yet to be concluded. While the death, mayhem, and destruction visited upon the inhabitants of two Japanese cities was barely hinted at, the dread of atomic warfare's ultimate results permeated even some of the proceedings' technical papers. Convictions that building the bomb was scientifically inevitable and an American-Soviet nuclear arms race a certainty shared the stage with expectations of both a future nuclear balance of terror and peaceful uses of atomic energy. Explicit and implicit in a number of presentations was criticism of existing governmental restrictions of scientific research and publication. Having listened to the symposium and discussing the need for freedom of research, the Society in executive session voted to send the following resolutions to President Truman (1946 *Year Book*, 46):

> WHEREAS, The growth of knowledge is an important source of the nation's strength, and whereas, the greatest freedom for study and discussion is essential to the effective growth of knowledge and of the national welfare, it is
>
> RESOLVED, That no legislation should interfere in any manner with basic scientific research and its publication in any field, and in particular with relation to atomic energy.

Meanwhile, the Library was making great strides under the leadership of William E. Lingelbach. His successor as Librarian Richard H. Shryock (APS 1944), the noted historian of American medicine, summed up Lingelbach's achievements concisely in 1963:

> When Dr. Lingelbach became Librarian of the American Philosophical Society in 1942, he was well known as an authority on modern European history and was already seventy-one years of age. Yet he then made for himself a second and quite distinct career, devoting himself for nearly two decades to the direction of the Library's operations and to the expansion of its holdings. Under his leadership, the Library assumed more of a role in the Society's affairs; and his faith in its future was finally realized by the construction of the new Library building. Few members have left such an imprint on the Society as did Dr. Lingelbach during years ordinarily devoted to retirement ("Lingelbach Biographical Memoir," 173).

Although Lingelbach had long been a member of the Committee on Library and in the early 1930s a leading advocate of the expansion of the social sciences and humanities in the Society, few would have predicted the achievements of his energetic "second career." True, Lingelbach had demonstrated an ability to work effectively and harmoniously with a wide variety of scholarly, civic, and social groups, but the challenges he faced — actually created for himself — were new to him. "Except for his general concern with the Philadelphia community, however, there was little in his previous experiences which would have suggested the great interest which he promptly displayed in everything pertaining to the Library" ("Lingelbach Biographical Memoir," 176). Lingelbach established the *Library Bulletin* (which later became an independent part of the annual *Proceedings*), appointed distinguished scholars as Library Research Associates who exploited the collection through research and stimulated interest in the institution generally, and he became a productive Franklin scholar and student of early Philadelphia history while devoting himself to the acquisition of Frankliniana, early American history, Native American collections, and the history of sciences. Lingelbach also made the Society central to the preservation movement that helped create the Independence State Mall and the Independence National Historical Park. This effort culminated in an Act of Congress in 1952 granting the Society permission to build a library building within the "Federal Mall." Erected on the old Library Company of Philadelphia site, Library Hall, was basically planned by Lingelbach. He retired as Librarian in 1957, but participated in laying the cornerstone a year later, and in 1959, "had the honor of formally presenting the building to the Society" on November 11, 1959 ("Lingelbach Biographical Memoir," 178).

During 1948-49, Philosophical Hall's exterior was restored to the pre-1890 state and its interior remodeled according to the plans of architect Paul Cret and modernized. The attractive marble stairway and semi-circular treatment of the walls on either side of the Fifth Street doorway, together with the colonial feeling of the Lecture (Meeting) Room, are examples of Cret's taste and respect for the old building. While demolition and construction was underway, the non-Library administrative functions were transferred to the Carl Schurz Memorial

Foundation in the Second Bank of the United States (Old Custom House). Portraits and busts were sent for exhibit to the Philadelphia Museum of Art, and for restoration. The balance of the fine and decorative arts, instruments, and memorabilia were divided between the Library in the Drexel Building and a storage company.

In April 1952, the Society voted to erect a library building in Independence National Historical Park. With nearly $2 million of construction and design funds safely in hand, and the federal government enthusiastically behind a project that would greatly enhance the Park at no direct cost to the taxpayers, the Society began serious planning of the modern Library. A memorial to Benjamin Franklin, the building was completed seven years later.

The American Philosophical Society was not content merely to honor its founder's memory in bricks and steel. In 1953, the Society joined with Yale University to undertake what may well prove to be its single greatest contribution to scholarship in modern times — a comprehensive edition of *The Papers of Benjamin Franklin*. Editors and a staff were selected, an office provided at Yale's Sterling Memorial Library, and also a temporary one at the Society, and on January 17, 1954 — the 248th anniversary of Franklin's birth — the project was announced. The Society, the holder of sixty five percent of known Franklin items, would contribute $410,000 over the years to the project. To date, twenty nine volumes spanning a period from Franklin's birth through the first third of his French ministry (June 30, 1779) have documented magnificently not only Franklin's life and career but also the creation of the American nation. Under the direction of four distinguished editors — Leonard W. Labaree (1953-69), William B. Willcox (1970-85), Claude A. Lopez (1985-86), and Barbara B. Oberg (1986-present) — the edition has received nearly universal critical acclaim, often being hailed as one of the great achievements of American historical scholarship of the twentieth century. All this lay ahead, but the course was well set when on

Fig. 13. Philosophical Hall after renovation of 1949.

November 11, 1959 during the Library Hall dedication ceremonies, "Roy F. Nichols (APS 1945) — Chairman of the Administrative Board of the Franklin Papers — announced that the Yale University Press had brought out the first volume of the Papers....Dr. Nichols commented on its significance to the Society in general and the Library in particular. In conclusion, he delivered a presentation copy to Dr. Henry Allen Moe (APS 1943) as President of the Society" (Shryock, "Planning Library Hall," 353). Moe accepted the volume with grace and wit — qualities he displayed further during his introductions of visiting dignitaries — later that evening during dinner at the aptly named Benjamin Franklin Hotel which culminated in the presentation of Library Hall to the Society.

Henry Allen Moe, President of the John Simon Guggenheim Foundation and for eleven years also President of the American Philosophical Society was one of the great talent scouts of scholarship, science, and the fine arts. During the First World War as a very young man, he won a naval commission and commanded a submarine chaser off the southeast coast of the United States. A shipboard accident fractured both his legs resulting in painful bone infections that plagued him for the balance of his life. He won a Rhodes scholarship, took two legal degrees at Oxford, studied further at the Inns of Court, became a barrister and lectured for a year at Balliol and Oriel Colleges.

Returning to America his real career began when Senator Simon Guggenheim asked him to help plan a foundation as a memorial to his son John Simon Guggenheim. For forty years Moe shaped and ran the foundation which became one of the nation's chief benefactors of creative scholars, scientists, and artists. Moe was deeply interested in people and had a keen critical sense of who would succeed and who would not in a reasonable length of time. He expanded the foundation's fellowship program to include novelists and poets, painters and photographers, composers, and choreographers. Moe's 1965 Cosmos Club Award citation stated: "He has selected some of the best of the avant-garde, while encouraging the solid

93

Fig. 14. Library Hall, 1985. Photography by Frank Margeson.

performances of veterans still capable of further accomplishment, standing ready to appoint an action painter or a twelve-tone composer or a nuclear physicist ("Moe Biographical Memoir," 106). The following year Henry Allen Moe became the first chairman of the National Endowment for the Humanities, a post he held for two years.

Moe brought qualities of humane critical judgment to his service as a member and Chairman of the Class III Committee on Membership, Chairman of the Advisory Committee on Membership, and, of course, his presidency of the Society. He was a master of bringing committees to a point of decision through tact and diplomacy. When all else failed and the decision too close to call, Moe would pronounce majestically — "I rule in the affirmative" or the negative as the case might be. He was proud to occupy Franklin's chair and brought a great deal of good sense, humor, and panache to the office. Moe's portrait by Franklin Watkins showing the subject resplendent in the scarlet robes of an honorary Oxford Doctor of Civil Laws hangs in the Library Reading Room. It is one of the Society's most intriguing paintings.

With Library Hall's new facilities and collections available, Librarian Richard H. Shryock began to hold a series of meetings that helped define the intellectual landscape of the history of science. During 1960-61, the Society and the American Physical Society formed a joint Committee on Theoretical Physics in the Twentieth Century to collect oral history and manuscript materials relating to the history of quantum physics. Under the leadership of Thomas S. Kuhn (APS 1974), then of the University of California, Berkeley, later Princeton, and now MIT, and with extensive National Science Foundation and institutional funding, the project flourished and became known as the Archives for the History of Quantum Physics. It was the first such synthetic archival enterprise to document key modern scientific developments. Today the Library continues to produce the 295 reels of microfilm "archive" that may be consulted at eighteen universities and research centers throughout the world. In September 1962, the Society served as co-host with Cornell to the Tenth International Congress of the History of Sciences held in Ithaca and Philadelphia.

President Julian P. Boyd (APS 1943) the founding editor of the modern edition of *The Papers of Thomas Jefferson* dedicated himself to the reformation of the Society's operations. During his presidency (1973-1976) the Society created an Executive Committee in 1975 that acts with the authority of the Councillors on important business between Council meetings. The following year Class V was established and a number of members transferred from other Classes to create a critical mass necessary to launch the new body.

The American Philosophical Society celebrated the Bicentennial of the United States at its Annual General Meeting in April 1976. Originally this was to be a much greater event. In 1965 plans began for a "Congress of Liberty," to which scholars and leaders from around the world were to be invited to discuss the current relevance of the Declaration of Independence to America and the world. The Congress was to take place in several sessions throughout the year, and also would feature a Philadelphia Orchestra performance of a Leonard Bernstein composition commissioned for the occasion. However, several national crises, including Watergate and rising inflation, created a less than ideal atmosphere for such activities. The Society reduced its ambitious plans and presented the Congress on a smaller scale as the topic of the April meeting. Meanwhile, in conjunction with the Historical Society of Pennsylvania and the Library Company of Philadelphia, the Society sponsored "A Rising People," a special exhibition of manuscripts illuminating the history of the American revolution which was regarded widely as one of the finest exhibits of the Bicentennial.

In April of the following year, an era came to an end with the retirement of the Society's first full-time Executive Officer, George Washington Corner (APS 1940), who had served with great distinction in that position since 1960 when he joined the staff at the age of seventy-one. George W. Corner continued as Editor of Publications and Chairman of the Committee on Research (two of the most demanding parts of his former job) for an additional three years, at which time he took his leave of the American Philosophical Society and went to live with his son in Alabama. A year later, in his ninety-second year, "Corner died quietly in his chair, in full possession to the last of his remarkable powers of intellect and personality" (1982 *Year Book*, 468). He had just completed the final tasks connected with the publication of his splendid, humane autobiography, *Seven Ages of a Medical Scientist*. As with all of George W. Corner's many, notable achievements, no loose ends remained.

Corner was born in Baltimore and received his undergraduate and medical education at The Johns Hopkins University. He served as a house officer in gynecology at Johns Hopkins Hospital before deciding on a career as a research scientist in anatomy that took him to the University of California, at Berkeley, back to Johns Hopkins, on to the University of Rochester, and then again to Baltimore as Director of the Department of Embryology of the Carnegie Institution of Washington (1940-55). He next spent five years in New York writing the history of the Rockefeller Institute which "was necessarily virtually a history of medical research in the United States in the first half of the twentieth century" (1981 *Year Book*, 466) before moving to Philadelphia to assume his duties in Philosophical Hall. Along the way George W. Corner made significant contributions to the study of the female reproductive cycle in the mammal and related endocrinology, helped his friend Dean George Hoyt Whipple (APS 1938) create one of America's great medical schools in Rochester from scratch, and wrote not only a valuable history of the Rockefeller Institute, but also of the University of Pennsylvania Medical School.

Corner, a man of great dignity and courtesy, brought to the position of Executive Officer unique administrative skills and common sense. He was an excellent planner with the ability to stick to timetables he developed for himself and his small staff. George W. Corner knew how the American Philosophical Society should function having been a Councillor, Vice President, and a member of the organization's major committees. He was always working but never rushed. With the assistance of Julia A. Noonan, Associate Secretary, Corner prepared committee meetings and the General Meetings skillfully, thus setting the stage for the Society's senior officers to execute not only regular business but major policy changes. "As in his research he was an innovator in his work with the Society, introducing a musical event to its program each year and streamlining the work of its office and of its various committees" (1982 *Year Book*, 467). Perhaps his most lasting contributions to the Society and the world of scholarship flowed from his extraordinary editorial skills and the care he lavished on publications.

The demands of the Executive Office were increasing steadily during Corner's final years. A larger staff to handle the work load and more modern budgetary and financial practices and controls clearly were required. The time had come for George W. Corner to step down and so at the age of eighty-eight with grace and good humor he did so. Today half of the resident membership remembers — most likely with affection — the American Philosophical Society of George Washington Corner while the balance knows that of his successors.

The Recent Leadership

As the officers involved in many of the Society's activities described in this section's opening pages are still very much a part of the current scene and any evaluation of their accomplishments might best be left to the future, these individuals will be identified with modest brevity. President Jonathan E. Rhoads (APS 1958) served from April 22, 1976 to April 21, 1984 when he was succeeded by President Crawford H. Greenewalt (APS 1954) whose three-year term was completed April 23, 1987. The second two-year term of President Eliot Stellar (APS 1977) will come to an end on April 30, 1993 during the 250th Anniversary Celebration. Whitfield J. Bell, Jr., (APS 1964) the only person to be both Librarian and Executive Officer, held the first office from 1966 through August 1980 and the second from 1977 through December 1983. Executive Officer Herman H. Goldstine (APS 1979) assumed his office on January 1, 1984, and Edward C. Carter II (APS 1983) became Librarian on September 1, 1980.

In the 1980s a number of distinguished women scholars and scientists such as Emily D. Townsend Vermeule (APS 1972) Harvard classicist and Greek Bronze Age specialist, Mabel L. Lang (APS 1971) Bryn Mawr professor of Greek, Jane M. Oppenheimer (APS 1980) Bryn Mawr biologist and historian of science, Mildred Cohn (APS 1972) Pennsylvania professor of physiological chemistry, Ruth Patrick (APS 1974) senior curator of limnology at the Academy of Natural Sciences, and Beatrice Mintz (APS 1982) senior member of the Fox Chase Institute for Cancer Research, claimed their rightful place as leaders of the American Philosophical Society. Some became officers of the organization, others powerful, long-term chairs of bodies like the Committee on Research.

Class V grew steadily and the dedication of its members to Society's mission was the equal of that of the other four Classes. That the Society could call on the services of two Class V members — George B. Beitzel (APS 1987) and Thomas J. Watson, Jr. (APS 1984) — to lead the Benjamin Franklin Hall campaign to a brilliant conclusion eloquently documents the Society's attractiveness to men and women of high achievement beyond the walls of the academy.

CORE ACTIVITIES: MEMBERSHIP AND MEETINGS, PUBLICATIONS, RESEARCH GRANTS, LIBRARY, AND COMMUNITY SERVICE

The American Philosophical Society is unique among learned societies for the open-handed, generous support it gives to the world of scholarship, the general public, and its membership. Over the years those closely associated with the Society have come to accept — indeed hardly give a second thought to — policies that subsidize research, publications, and meetings to an extraordinary degree. One of the great things about the Library, for example, (so accepted by members and staff that it is not thought remarkable), is its accessibility to any

Fig. 15. Benjamin Franklin Hall, 1984. Photography by Frank Margeson.

serious reader. There is no charge for admission, no serious limitations on the use of collections, inexpensive reproductive fees, expert staff advice, and the opportunity for research support — all so different from most sister institutions. Every other activity of the Society can boast of analogous services offered.

The Society's 1992 budget of $3.7 million was allocated to its major core activities as follows: membership and meetings $300,898; publications $492,524; research grants $773,883, and library services $1.4 million. The balance of some $712,150 was devoted to general administrative expenses.

By April 1992, approximately 3,450 resident members had been elected to the Society since its founding in 1743. Of these, 113 members had been removed from the rolls mainly between 1850 and 1930 when those living within thirty miles of Philosophical Hall or other members wishing to vote in elections paid an admission fee and an annual one thereafter. Forfeiture of membership resulted from non-payment of dues for three years. The Society's membership files generally throw little light on resignations. Old age and/or infirmity which preclude participation in the Society's affairs and a disinclination to pay dues any longer were the basic reasons for surrendering membership. Since fees and dues were suspended in the mid-1930s, there apparently had been no resignations — although three persons declined election during these years.

The past decade has seen a growing interest in and support of the Society by a significant portion of both the resident and foreign members. This trend most likely has been caused by a combination of factors: the two successful Benjamin Franklin Hall construction and fund-raising campaigns, the joint Royal Society meetings, the establishment of the Society newsletter, and the prospect of the 250th Anniversary Celebration. Whatever the reasons the results are to be seen in the members' impressive financial support of the two capital campaigns and the annual Friends of the Library contributions, their voluntary submission of informative items for the newsletter, and a new-found willingness to complete their Society biographical files. All this augurs well for the Society's future.

Members are elected to the Society in recognition of signal contributions to important fields of human endeavor. They number 690 worldwide, the majority being professional scholars of high distinction, but including equally distinguished leaders in other fields. All are expected to possess and cherish, in the words of the Society's charter of 1780, "a humane and philosophical spirit," and to manifest a devotion to the public good. Of all the men and women throughout the world who have received Nobel Prizes, thirty percent are or have been members of the Society. Nearly two-thirds were elected to the Society before they became Nobel laureates. Naturally, mathematicians, social scientists, and humanities scholars have received comparable awards and distinctions in their respective disciplines. Other members, in the Jeffersonian tradition, are leaders in the arts, business and the professions, or in public service.

Although many continue to regard the Society as principally a scientific organization, today social scientists and humanists comprise fifty percent of the Society's resident membership. One measure of this group's contribution to American and international learning is that twelve of the twenty-two NEH Jefferson Lectures in the Humanities have been presented by members of the Society. These renowned scholars and creative artists are not merely names on the Society's rolls but, almost without exception, they have been and are active, working, contributing members who serve as officers or on committees and present numerous papers at Society meetings.

Meetings of the Society are concentrated and intense, and are designed to stimulate thinking and discussion through the frequent presentation of conflicting views. In a two to three-day period twice yearly anywhere between twelve and twenty papers are presented and discussed, sometimes heatedly, often with the result that new research is undertaken. In recent years, the programs have seen a return to an earlier tradition — the inclusion of symposia on critical, current issues.

As it has done since 1771, when the first volume of its *Transactions* appeared, the Society publishes an array of scholarly books, monographs and articles. Every year, one volume of *Proceedings* and another of *Transactions* appears, each containing articles and short monographs. Additionally, five to eight volumes of *Memoirs* are published annually, each a full-length book on a separate subject. Early volumes of the *Proceedings* and *Transactions* reported on the biological, geological and astronomical observations and discoveries by Society members and others. In this century, the scope of both publications has been enlarged to include research papers and monographs by scholars from throughout the United States and the world. *Memoirs* recently projected or published are on such widely diverse subjects as the transformation of Latin into Spanish, long-lost British parliamentary proceedings dating back to 1614, medieval medicine, ancient Egyptian science, a study of Biblical tracts translated into Indian languages, the mysterious lines of Nazca, Peru, and the relation of Christendom to Islam in the period from 1204 to 1571. The authors of the *Transactions* are, typically, young post-doctoral students who are anxious to obtain publication of their first research. The authors of the *Memoirs* are generally well-established scholars whose works are in such specialized fields that even university presses will not underwrite their publication.

In 1933, the Society became one of the first private independent organizations to establish an ongoing program of grants to assist the research of individual scholars and investigators. Since the first grant was made to Dr. Thomas C. Poulter of the Second Byrd Antarctic Expedition for his work in measuring the depth of the polar ice cap, the Society has awarded more than $15 million to support research by over 12,000 scholars. Many of these grants are made principally to support the cost of travel to distant points where research is to be conducted. This is essential since few funding agencies provide such resources. Among recipients of these grant funds have been Lyman H. Butterfield, (APS 1964) for his edition of *The Letters of Benjamin Rush*; Tracy Sonneborn, (APS 1952) for research on sex inheritance and determination in ciliate protozoa; Samuel Noah

Fig. 16. April 1986 American Philosophical Society-Royal Society Joint Meeting. View looking south at luncheon tent in Jefferson Garden with Library Hall behind. Photography by Frank Margeson.

Fig. 17. Executive Officer Herman H. Goldstine welcoming members and guests at luncheon during American Philosophical Society-Royal Society Joint Meeting.

Kramer, (APS 1949) for research on the Sumerians; Herbert Gans, for studies of suburban life; and Loren C. Eiseley, (APS 1960) for research for *Darwin's Century*. Special endowments support projects in clinical medicine, silviculture and the progress of agriculture in the United States. Among the more than one hundred recipients in the field of clinical medicine have been Victor A. McKusick, (APS 1975) for investigation of different types of hereditary dystrophy of connective tissue, and David W. Fraser for the examination of the interplay of host defenses in immunologically impaired hosts as they relate to the development of clinical disease. Among the eight recipients supported in the field of silviculture and related studies have been institutions like the Morris Arboretum of the University of Pennsylvania and the Gray Herbarium of Harvard University. Other special grant programs support research in Native American linguistics and ethnohistory, in the collections of the Library, and dissertations in the history of modern physical sciences.

The Library of the American Philosophical Society is one of the world's leading centers for research in the history of science and of early American culture. The quality of its holdings in its particular fields ranks with those of its sister independent libraries — the Folger, the Morgan, and the Huntington. Open to the public without charge, the Library serves investigators in many disciplines who come from around the country — and increasingly from foreign countries as well — to study in its collection of 180,000 books and 6 million manuscripts. Computer technology has been applied to cataloging and other aspects of its management, and a modern paper conservation facility was completed in 1987. Outstanding examples of early materials in the collections are papers and personal books of Benjamin Franklin, the letters and sketches of Charles Willson Peale and his family, the journals of Lewis and Clark and some 800 letters of Charles Darwin. More recent work is represented by the papers of the anthropologist Franz Boas, the paleontologist

George Gaylord Simpson, the geneticist Theodosius Dobzhansky, and the mathematician Stanislaw Ulam. The Library also promotes scholarship by providing administrative support and/or funding support for a wide range and variety of research project, such as *The Papers of Benjamin Franklin, The Joseph Henry Papers, The Correspondence of Charles Darwin,* and *The Papers of Benjamin Henry Latrobe,* the architect. All these are works now in progress. Conferences on topics as diverse as the history of modern physics and the demography of Philadelphia are sponsored regularly by the Library. Fellowship stipends and periodically updated bibliographies help facilitate the use of the Library by researchers, while public exhibitions and summer seminars for high school teachers interpret the collections to a wider audience.

An organization devoted to learning must teach respect for learning and an understanding of its fundamental importance in a free society. Moreover, an organization functioning at the center of a major urban area and in the heart of Independence National Historical Park must also be a good neighbor and play an active role in the shared life of its neighborhood. To accomplish these ends, the Society opens its doors to its friends, neighbors and visitors, invites them to attend its semi-annual meetings, to use its library resources, to see historical scientific exhibits and artifacts, and to use its facilities for a wide array of professional and social gatherings. In addition the Society participates in a number of programs in support of the secondary schools, colleges and universities in the region. These include PATHS (Philadelphia Alliance for the Teaching of the Humanities in the Schools), PRISM (Philadelphia Renaissance in Science and Mathematics), University of Pennsylvania undergraduate and graduate history programs, conservation internships for students at the University of the Arts, conservation workshops for staffs of small libraries and historical societies, and the teaching of library skills in selected secondary schools of the Philadelphia Public School System. Finally it should be noted that the Library, its

Fig. 18. President Eliot Stellar and Librarian Edward C. Carter II in Library Reading Room thanking the Friends of the Library for their generous annual support at a recent November Friends Reception. Photography by Frank Margeson.

collections and staff serve as an adjunct research facility for Park Service researchers.

Things To Come

What will the American Philosophical Society look like fifty years hence during its Tricentennial? If past experience can be a guide, the resident membership probably will be 800 or more in 2043. Certainly it will be more diverse reflecting the gender and minority distribution of major research universities' faculties, if not the general population. There will be one or more additional classes to accommodate new disciplines and currently unrepresented interdisciplinary scholarship. The Society most likely will carry out its traditional core functions certainly utilizing new technologies such as advanced teleconferencing which will allow greater geographical representation on committees and encourage younger members in mid-career to participate more actively in the Society's deliberations.

Benjamin Franklin Hall with its auditorium and related facilities provides the Society with splendid opportunities for service beyond the two Annual General Meetings. The completion of the nearby Pennsylvania Convention Center in 1993 and the dramatic increase of hotel rooms means that the city once again will become a major center for large-scale professional, scholarly, and commercial meetings. It is conceivable that joint meetings might be held with other learned organizations like the American Historical Association or the National Academy of Sciences as was done formerly. Benjamin Franklin Hall already has been made available by the Society for the annual meetings of the Association of Documentary Editors (October 1993) and the American Council of Learned Societies (April 1994). Benjamin Franklin Hall also will allow the Society to play a much more active and influential role in Philadelphia's educational and cultural community. The new auditorium — the only modern, comfortable facility of its kind and size in the Independence Hall area — will be made available on a reservation basis to neighboring cultural bodies like the Pennsylvania Horticultural Society, the Afro-American Historical and Cultural Museum, the Atwater Kent Museum of Philadelphia History, the Annenberg Research Institute for Judaic and Near Eastern Studies, the Athenaeum of Philadelphia, and the Library Company of Philadelphia. The attractive ambience, advanced audiovisual technology, and historical setting will make Benjamin Franklin Hall a much sought after meeting site.

What benefits might accrue to the Society from such neighborly hospitality? At the very basic level it would allow the Society to enlarge a practice that has been followed in Philosophical Hall and the Library for many years. A key part of the Society's mission has always been assisting sister institutions and groups in the promotion of their scholarly and social activities. The beautiful auditorium will give greater exposure to such contributions and enhance the reputation of the Society locally, nationally, and even internationally. Benjamin Franklin Hall also will increase the opportunities for cooperative programs with other organizations such as consortia of regional colleges and universities and public bodies like the School District of Philadelphia with which we have an on-going tradition of assisting in teacher education and enrichment. Exhibitions on the history and work of the American Philosophical Society in the Fels Room adjacent to the Chestnut Street entrance will provide an opportunity to tell the Society's story to a much wider audience than formerly. Hopefully potential donors and interested foundation officials will appreciate such generous institutional activities when the Society concentrates — as it must soon — on the need to enlarge significantly the endowment of its key programs.

The Society has already responded to the criticism that its meetings' papers are occasionally too general and do not always reflect the most current scholarship by revamping the format of the Jayne Lectures. In recent years, specialists have spoken about their latest research to small gatherings which purposely include a significant number of their non-Society peers. This program will be expanded in scope and number to reach wider professional and lay audiences. Another strategy would be to emulate the Midwinter Meetings of the late 1930s and early 1940s featuring highly focused disciplinary symposia coupled with rapid publication of the papers and discussions. The Society has generally shied away from public policy discussion because of its tradition of not taking stands on issues that might be considered political. The availability of Benjamin Franklin Hall, the Society's prestige and reputation for evenhandedness, and the expertise to be found in the membership may well argue for the Society to sponsor public policy forums devoted to critical local, national, and international problems. Impressive precedents can be found in recent general meetings that brought together leading authorities to examine challenging topics like immigration and the American underclass.

The Society's physical facilities now are excellent and should take care of most requirements for the next fifty years. Library Hall will have to be partially retrofitted before the end of the century. The climate control system is as old as the building itself and in recent years the temperature and humidity balance has been unacceptable occasionally in certain parts of the building. The only long-term solution is a new climate control system for which funds are being set aside. A modern sprinkler system capable of extinguishing fires with a minimum of water damage to collections should be installed throughout the building. Space below and above the Thomas Jefferson Garden to the north of the Library will remain available to satisfy the Society's far-distant building requirements.

Hail But Not Farewell

This account of the American Philosophical Society's first 250 years may properly conclude with words President Frederick Fraley spoke at the conclusion of the Society's Sesquicentennial a hundred years ago. The sole survivor of the Society's Centennial of 1843, Fraley was President from 1880 until his death at the age of ninety seven in 1901. The friendly and optimistic sentiments expressed are those of a man who had lived through half a century of the Society's history. That Frederick Fraley had witnessed times of institutional hope and despair, the horrors of the Civil War, and the Centennial of American Independence that celebrated the resumption of national union and material progress lends a quality of moral poignancy to his message. His words are no less appropriate today; they may, it is to be hoped, not only touch the mystic cords of memory but also heighten the Society's present and future expectations.

> The programme for the celebration of our 150th anniversary is now literally completed. I cannot say farewell to you, for what I have felt here in meeting so many new and so many old friends does not permit me to entertain the thought that I must part from them. All I can say is that we have been signally blessed in this celebration. We have not only had a perpetuation of good words and perpetuation of good cheer, but the beginning of friendships which will last certainly so long as we are permitted to tread the earth. I thank you all for what has been given to us upon this occasion, hoping, as Professor George F. Barker (APS 1873) has expressed the hope, that the good work for the promotion of science will go on for a series and series and series of 150 years; that not only our own institution may take its part in the great work

113

of promoting useful knowledge, but all the institutions that are represented here and all others who are not and have tendered their congratulations will equally continue at work, and that those who come, I will say 150 years hence, but I will shorten the period and say all those who may come here fifty years hence, will find the old hall standing on its foundation with accumulated treasures within its walls and precious memories encircling the hearts of all those who have been in the past members of the Society and who are now its present members, all those who have been correspondents of the Society in the past and are present correspondents, and that it will be followed by a perpetuity of existence and a perpetuity of correspondence that will endure forever.

So I shall not say farewell, but I will announce that so far as I am concerned this body shall be continued in session until another fifty years roll around, and ask that you will make the advent of such a coming a welcome to every one.

ADJOURNED.

Sources Cited

Cyrus Adler to Horace C. Richards, July 26, 1927. Building and Endowment Campaign File. American Philosophical Society Archives.

Bell, Whitfield J., Jr. "The American Philosophical Society as a National Academy of Sciences, 1780-1846." Tenth International Congress of the History of Science, *Proceedings* (Paris, 1962), 165-175.

_____. "As Others Saw Us: Notes on the Reputation of the American Philosophical Society." American Philosophical Society, *Proceedings* 166 (1972):269-278.

Bonner, J.T. and Bell, Whitfield J., Jr. "'What is Money For?': An Interview with Edwin Grant Conklin, 1952." American Philosophical Society, *Proceedings* 128 (1984):79-83.

Brownlee, David B. *Building the City Beautiful: The Benjamin Franklin Parkway and the Philadelphia Museum of Art.* Philadelphia: Philadelphia Museum of Art, 1989.

Bruce, Robert V. *The Launching of Modern American Science 1846-1876.* New York: Alfred A. Knopf, 1987.

"Edwin G. Conklin Biographical Memoir." American Philosophical Society, 1952 *Year Book* (1953):4-12.

John Price Jones Corporation Memorandum, [May 16, 1930]. Building and Endowment Campaign File. American Philosophical Society Archives.

Kammen, Michael. *Mystic Chords of Memory: The Transformation of Tradition in American Culture.* New York: Alfred A. Knopf, 1991.

"William E. Lingelbach Biographical Memoir." American Philosophical Society, 1963 *Year Book* (1964):173-179.

Lingelbach, William E. "Philosophical Hall: The Home of the American Philosophical Society." *Historic Philadelphia: From the Founding until the Early Nineteenth Century,* edited by Luther P. Eisenhart. American Philosophical Society, *Transactions* 43 (1953):43-69.

Mankind Advancing: A Message of Progress. Philadelphia: American Philosophical Society, 1929.

"Henry Allen Moe Biographical Memoir." American Philosophical Society, 1976 *Year Book (*1977):103-109.

"Roland S. Morris Biographical Memoir." American Philosophical Society, 1945 *Year Book* (1946):389-398.

A Plea for the American Philosophical Society and its Need of a New Building to be known as "Franklin House." [Philadelphia: American Philosophical Society, 1913.]

Report of a Special Committee on a Site for a New Hall. Philadelphia: American Philosophical Society, May 1, 1911.

Shryock, Richard H. "The Planning and Formal Opening of Library Hall." American Philosophical Society, *Proceedings* 104 (1960) :349-356.

Sketch of The Wistar Party of Philadelphia. Being a reprint of the edition of 1846 with a continuation to the present time. Philadelphia: 1898. [Reprinted with a continuation to 1976].

Selected Bibliography

Baatz, Simon. "Patronage, Science, and Ideology in an American City: Patrician Philadelphia, 1800-1860." Ph.D. diss., University of Pennsylvania, 1986.

Bell, Whitfield J., Jr. "The Scientific Environment of Philadelphia, 1775-1790." American Philosophical Society, *Proceedings* 92 (1948):6-14.

A Catalogue of Portraits and other Works of Art in the Possession of the American Philosophical Society. American Philosophical Society, *Memoirs* 54 (1961).

Chinard, Gilbert. "The American Philosophical Society and the World of Science, 1768-1800." American Philosophical Society, *Proceedings* 87 (1943):1-11.

Du Ponceau, Peter Stephen. *An Historical Account of the Origin and Formation of the American Philosophical Society.* Philadelphia: American Philosophical Society, 1914.

Early Proceedings of the American Philosophical Society ... compiled ... from the Manuscript Minutes of Its Meetings from 1744 to 1838. Philadelphia: 1884.

Greene, John C. *American Science in the Age of Jefferson.* Ames: Iowa State University Press, 1984.

Gross, Walter Elliot. "The American Philosophical Society and the Growth of Science in the United States: 1835-1850." Ph.D. diss., University of Pennsylvania, 1970.

Hindle, Brooke. *The Pursuit of Science in Revolutionary America.* Chapel Hill: University of North Carolina Press, 1956.

_____. "The Rise of the American Philosophical Society, 1766 to 1787." Ph.D. diss., University of Pennsylvania, 1949.

Multhauf, Robert P. *A Catalogue of Instruments and Models in the Possession of the American Philosophical Society.* American Philosophical Society, *Memoirs* 53 (1961).

Smith, Murphy D. *Oak from an Acorn: A History of the American Philosophical Society Library, 1770-1803.* Wilmington, DE.: Scholarly Resources, Inc., 1976.

Vaughan, John. "An Account of the American Philosophical Society (1841)." Philadelphia: Friends of the Library, American Philosophical Society, 1972.